BAKE IT YOURSELF

BIY

BIY
BAKE IT YOURSELF

Rach,

Happy Baking!

Richard

RICHARD BURR

QUADRILLE

For Sarah, Elizabeth and Genevieve

Publishing director: Sarah Lavelle
Creative director: Helen Lewis
Copy editor: Lucy Bannell
Design: Two Associates
Photography: Chris Terry
Food styling: Richard Burr, Emily Jonzen, Rukmini Iyer
Props stylist: Polly Webb-Wilson
Production: Vincent Smith, Emily Noto

First published in 2015 by
Quadrille Publishing Limited
Pentagon House
52–54 Southwark Street
London SE1 1UN

www.quadrille.co.uk

Quadrille is an imprint of Hardie Grant
www.hardiegrant.com.au

Text © Richard Burr 2015
Photography © Chris Terry 2015
Design and layout © Quadrille Publishing Limited 2015

Cataloguing in Publication Data: a catalogue record for
this book is available from the British Library.

ISBN: 978 1 84949 699 5

Printed in China

CONTENTS

INTRODUCTION 6

TOOL KIT 8

1. BREAD 10

2. SWEET DOUGH 30

3. CAKES 48

4. CELEBRATION CAKES 68

5. BISCUITS 88

6. SAVOURY PIES 108

7. SWEET PIES 124

8. TARTS 138

9. SAVOURY PASTRIES 154

10. SWEET PASTRIES 172

11. PUDDINGS 192

12. BASICS 210

ACKNOWLEDGEMENTS 218

INDEX 220

INTRODUCTION

When I first stepped into the *Bake Off* tent last year, I thought they had made some sort of administrative error and would take one look at me and send me home with an apology and a free bag of sugar. Luckily for me, they felt like taking a punt on a builder, so I made the most of it and things turned out pretty well.

My route into home baking was much the same as for a lot of people. I was brought up in a home where both my mum and dad cooked regularly – not fancy food, but great, home-made meals. I learned how to cook by being given simple things to do, such as peeling the carrots or sticking bread in the toaster, and was gradually allowed more responsibility in the kitchen as I became more competent.

When I was 15, and still not big enough to make it on to building sites with my Dad, I got a job in a local bakery; mainly washing up and carrying baked goods from the kitchens to the shop (and scrumping a few along the way). I was very lucky to have this job; my mates either had paper rounds or worked at shop counters. As a teenager, to be around while real, skilled craftsmen plied their trade was a goldmine of information! Every now and again I'd be allowed to cook and fill the doughnuts, or jam and ice the Danish pastries, but mainly I paid a lot of attention to the baker, David Anstee, as he whipped up a sticky croquembouche tower or knocked out a perfect batch of fondant fancies.

Anyway, fast forward a good few years and I built my own kitchen to cover in flour without my mum getting upset at the mess. I tried hard to remember the hints and tips I had picked up all those years ago, but I wasn't particularly good at baking. The passion remained, however and, after a few years, I began to improve. I started to iron out my mistakes, find flavours that worked and experiment with new ingredients. When I became a dad, my wife Sarah and I would stay up late into the night before each daughter's birthday making increasingly extravagant cakes. My bakes got better and more varied, and friends and family started to comment: 'You should go on that *Bake Off*...'

This book is full of my favourite bakes. I've learned in my own kitchen and made plenty of blunders, so that you don't have to make them yourself. I haven't been formally trained, so I've tried to avoid any baker's jargon and explain everything step by step from one home baker to another. I've stuck to familiar ingredients wherever I can, but have included others to swap in or out if you want to make your bakes more or less exotic; you should be able to get two or three variations out of each recipe. I've divided each chapter into beginner, intermediate and advanced sections (levels 1, 2 and 3), to accommodate every sort of home baker.

Last but not least, thank you for buying my book! I really hope you enjoy it and feel encouraged to work your way through the levels and experiment with things you never thought you'd be able to bake yourself.

Happy baking!

Richard

TOOL KIT

Over the years I've accumulated quite a lot of baking kit. I buy most of it online, as I find it easier to find exactly what I'm looking for. The five items I can't live without these days are:

1. stand mixer (I managed for years without one but, now I have it, I use it all the time – it's a real investment)

2. silicone spatulas

3. offset palette knife

4. dough scraper

5. accurate digital scales

Some of the additional kit I use in the book is listed below. You don't need all of it, but this list might be good to leave lying around as a heavy hint before your next birthday or Christmas. I've also given an equipment list in each recipe to let you know what you might need.

ELECTRICAL KIT

- electric whisk
- deep-fat fryer (optional, but if you're as much of a doughnut addict as me, it's pretty essential)
- food processor (optional)

TINS AND TRAYS

- 2 baking sheets
- large and small roasting tins
- Swiss roll tin (about 33 x 23cm)
- large Swiss roll tin (about 40 x 27cm)
- 900g loaf tin
- 18cm square or adjustable cake tin (the latter is a really useful tin to have)
- 2 x 20cm round sandwich tins
- 23cm round deep-sided sandwich tin
- 23cm springform cake tin
- 23cm loose-bottomed tart tin
- 22cm shallow pie tin or dish
- 26cm rectangular pie dish with rim
- 24cm deep-sided, round metal pie dish
- small baking tin (about 23 x 15cm)
- ovenproof dish (about 27 x 23cm)
- 12-hole muffin tin
- 6 x 10cm loose-bottomed tartlet tins
- 6 ramekins
- 6 mini pudding moulds
- 6 x 6cm diameter presentation rings
- Bundt tin
- panettone tin

ACCESSORIES

- rolling pin (I have a standard pin and an adjustable rolling pin for rolling dough out to a specific thickness)
- wire cooling racks
- cooking/confectionery thermometer
- pastry brush
- flavour injector (essential if you love doughnuts)
- disposable piping bags
- various icing nozzles: large star-tipped nozzle, 2mm nozzle, long-nosed nozzle, 15mm round nozzle (and I tend to pick up interesting-looking ones when I'm out and about; I have a tinful…)
- cake/icing smoother
- different-sized mixing bowls
- heatproof bowl (for melting chocolate)
- measuring jug
- measuring spoons
- various cutters: round, fluted and of different diameters (2cm, 3cm, 6cm, 8cm, 9cm), plus novelty cutters (such as star- or heart-shaped)
- cook's blow torch (not essential, but always fun to play with)
- cake-cutting wire (not essential, but useful)
- baking beans (ditto)
- pie bird (again, not essential, but great for making your pie look like it's been drawn in a story book)

INGREDIENTS

Eggs
I always use free-range large eggs. I used to cook with the eggs from my dad's chickens, but they're not uniform in size so now I save those for fried/boiled/poached/scrambled and only bake with large eggs.

Flour
I always use own-brand supermarket flour. I know a lot of bakers suggest higher-end flours, but I've never had a problem with the more affordable bags.

Food colour
I tend to use gel colours: they last longer, are more concentrated and produce more vivid colours without adding extra liquid to the mix. I buy them online; I particularly like those made by Wilton.

Salt
I use table salt in all yeasted dough recipes, unless otherwise specified.

Water
I measure mine in ml; some other people weigh it (because 1ml water = 1g). I don't tend to use lukewarm water in yeasted recipes, except where specified. I just don't usually find it necessary.

Yeast
Wherever I've mentioned yeast in the book, I've used Doves Farm Quick Yeast.

BREAD

PIZZA

I have kids. Pizza is therefore twice as expensive as it used to be, because even though the two new people in our family are pretty tiny, it's amazing how much they can put away. I much prefer these pizzas to the greasy, heavy takeaway variety and I think you will, too. The dough is easy to make and the pizzas are quick to cook. At our house on a Saturday night I make a couple of bases and we all pile in and top them with whatever we want. The kids are happy, and so am I.

MAKES 2 BASES

Ingredients

For the pizza bases

300g strong white bread flour,
    plus more to dust
½ tsp table salt
1 tbsp 'quick' yeast
1 tsp caster sugar
190ml water
1 tbsp olive oil, plus more for
    the bowl

For the pizza sauce

150ml tomato passata
15g basil leaves,
    finely chopped
1 garlic clove, crushed
sea salt and freshly ground
    black pepper

Suggested toppings

black olives
ball of mozzarella cheese,
    chopped into small pieces
yellow pepper, sliced
salami slices
10g basil leaves
handful of grated
    Cheddar cheese

Tool Kit

rolling pin
2 large baking sheets or
    baking trays

1. Make the dough by combining the dry ingredients in a bowl with a wooden spoon, making sure you put the salt and yeast in opposite sides of the bowl (if you pop one on top of the other, the salt will kill the yeast). Add the water and the 1 tbsp of olive oil. Mix until the flour comes away from the sides, then tip on to a floured surface. Knead for 5–10 minutes, or until smooth and elastic. Rub a few drops of oil around the bowl you used, pop the dough back in it, cover with cling film and leave for 1 hour at room temperature.

2. Meanwhile, make the sauce. Pour the passata into a saucepan and add the basil and garlic. Add salt and pepper to taste and gently bring to the boil, then reduce the heat and simmer for 5 minutes only, to retain the fresh tomato taste. Take off the heat to cool.

3. Once the dough has risen, take it out of the bowl, give it a quick knead to knock out the air, and halve it. Make each base by rolling a piece of the dough out on a lightly floured work surface, using a rolling pin, to a 25cm circle or thereabouts. If you want to be a bit flash, you can pick up a base and toss it up in the air, spinning it. Catch the dough on the back of your hand, so your fingers don't poke through. Do this at least 3 times to achieve a thin centre and a thicker outer crust. (The kids love the display!)

4. Lay each base on a piece of baking parchment and cover the top with another piece of baking parchment, then set aside for 15 minutes. Repeat the process with the second piece of dough. Preheat the oven to 240°C/fan 220°C/gas 9 and place 2 large baking sheets inside. (If you don't have baking sheets, you can put baking trays in upside down and use the bottoms of the trays to bake the pizzas.)

5. After the bases have rested, remove the top layer of parchment, spread the sauce evenly over them and add your toppings.

6. Take the baking sheets out of the oven and quickly put on the pizzas, still on their lower layer of baking parchment. (You won't get soggy bottoms as long as the baking sheets are piping hot.) Place in the oven and cook for 10 minutes. Take out, slice and eat immediately!

Extras

At home we like to crack an egg on to the pizza halfway through cooking.

You can make a pizza into a calzone by topping it, then flipping over half of it to make a 'pasty' shape. Stick the edges together with some beaten egg, though, or the calzone will leak the filling all over your oven.

SIMPLE WHITE BLOOMER

If you're just starting to Bake It Yourself, there's no better building block than basic white bread. Few things are more appealing than the aroma of a freshly baked loaf wafting through your house. When I started baking, I mucked up lots of loaves by over-complicating them, but I've since learned that there's no need. With this recipe, you will achieve a great-tasting loaf first time around and see how incredibly simple it is to make.

MAKES 1 LOAF
Ingredients
500g strong white bread flour, plus more to dust
1 tbsp 'quick' yeast
2 tsp table salt
2 tbsp olive oil, plus more for the bowl
300ml water

Tool Kit
baking tray
small roasting tin
wire cooling rack

1. Stick the flour in a large bowl. Add the yeast to one side of the bowl and the salt to the other and mix with a wooden spoon. Add the 2 tbsp of oil and the water and continue to mix, using the spoon at first, then, once it stops looking sticky, your hands, until all the flour has come away from the sides; this dough should leave the bowl pretty clean.

2. Tip out on to a lightly floured surface and knead for 10 minutes. Once the dough is smooth, rub a few drops of oil around the bowl, pop the dough back in it, cover with cling film and leave at room temperature for 1–2 hours until it has at least doubled in size. It is worth taking a photo of it on your phone so you can compare later to see whether it's risen enough. If you're feeling impatient, stick it somewhere warm (such as the airing cupboard). You'll still make a nice loaf but it won't be as flavoursome. (That's because flavour develops as a yeasted dough proves, so speeding up the process means you miss out on some of that extra taste.)

3. Once it's proved, tip out the dough on to a very lightly floured surface and 'knock back', by folding it in on itself about 6 or 7 times to pop the large air bubbles. Pat into a long oval shape, about 25cm long, and put on to a baking tray lined with baking parchment. Put the tray inside a plastic carrier bag – the bag shouldn't touch the dough but should form a tent around it – and leave it to prove again for 1 hour.

4. Preheat the oven to 240°C/fan 220°C/gas 9, fill a small roasting tin with around 200ml of boiling water and put it in the bottom of the oven (this will help to form a crunchy crust on the loaf).

5. Remove the dough from the plastic bag and, with a very sharp knife, slash the loaf diagonally at 2cm intervals along the top, then dust lightly with flour.

6. Bake for 30–35 minutes until a rich brown colour. To check the loaf is done, turn it upside down and tap the base; it will sound hollow when it is cooked. Leave on a cooling rack until cold.

KNEADING

Everyone kneads differently, but the most important thing is to stretch the dough. I push the heel of my palm into the centre of the dough, squishing it down, then push it away. The dough flattens out and I fold it back over, turn the dough, then repeat. It doesn't seem like it'll happen at first, but the dough does eventually change from lumpy and rough to smooth and elastic. Once it's smooth, give it a few minutes' more kneading, as you can't over-knead by hand and it's the closest thing you get to exercising in the kitchen! I normally take about 10 minutes to knead, but it may take slightly longer until you get the hang of it.

Extras

Nice one! You just made bread. Now, here are a few ways to muck about with it:

Shape the loaf in different ways: form a round 'cob' with a cross slashed in the middle; or make a 'sandwich' loaf by putting the dough in a standard-sized (900g) loaf tin before its second proving.

Before it goes into the oven, instead of dusting with flour, you can spray water on the top of the loaf and sprinkle with poppy seeds or sesame seeds.

This dough can also be plaited; have a play with it and see what you come up with.

Pictured overleaf: *(top left)* Simple white bloomer; *(bottom left)* Seeded wholemeal rolls (see page 18); *(right)* Black olive and rosemary breadsticks (see page 19).

SEEDED WHOLEMEAL ROLLS

Now, I'm not going to lie to you: not everything in this book is entirely good for you in large quantities. This recipe has no such problems. These rolls are not only delicious, but are packed with healthy oils and fibre, so make them, eat them and feel smug in the knowledge that you've done your bit today. Personally, I like to fill them with cheese and bacon, but I suppose there's no helping some people...

MAKES 8
Ingredients
500g strong wholemeal bread
   flour, plus more to dust
2 tsp table salt
1 tbsp 'quick' yeast
50g unsalted butter, in
   small cubes
50g pumpkin seeds
3 tbsp sunflower seeds
2 tbsp sesame seeds
2 tbsp poppy seeds
350ml water

Tool Kit
baking tray
wire cooling rack

1. Put the flour, salt, yeast and butter in a bowl, making sure you add the salt and yeast to opposite sides of the bowl, then mix with a wooden spoon. Add all the seeds and mix again. Add the water and stir together until the flour has come away from the bowl.

2. Tip out on to a floured surface and knead for 5–10 minutes until the dough becomes stretchy. The bigger seeds will fall out a lot during the kneading, but just keep poking them back in.

3. Once the dough is stretchy and as smooth as dough filled with hundreds of seeds can be, place in a bowl, cover with cling film and leave at room temperature for about 2 hours until doubled or trebled in size. You might want to take a quick picture on your phone to check later how your rise is going.

4. Tip the risen dough on to a lightly floured work surface and knock back by folding the dough in on itself 6 or 7 times. Allow the dough to rest for 5 minutes, then cut it into 8 pieces by halving, then halving again, then again... or if you're feeling particularly precise you can weigh the dough and divide the total by 8.

5. Roll the 8 portions of dough into balls and place on a baking tray lined with baking parchment. Cover with a plastic bag – the bag shouldn't touch the rolls but should form a tent around them – and leave to rise for about 1 hour.

6. Once risen, preheat the oven to 240°C/fan 220°C/gas 9, cut crosses in each roll with scissors and lightly sprinkle with flour.

7. Bake for 15–20 minutes or until the rolls sound hollow when tapped on the base. Remove from the oven and set on a wire rack to cool.

Extras
These rolls work very well with any type of filling. The seed combo I've given here is one of my wife's favourites, but feel free to add whatever you like:

Coarse-chopped walnuts are always a good choice, but make sure you use fresh-bought nuts, not the half-bag mouldering in the back of the cupboard.

Other options are sun-dried tomatoes, olives, bits of dried fig, anything really, although if you are adding wet ingredients, don't add all the water in one go; start with about 300ml and see how your dough comes together from there.

I like to put a lump of Roquefort or Dolcelatte inside and bake my rolls with the cheese already in them. It opens the door to loads more flavour combinations.

BLACK OLIVE AND ROSEMARY BREADSTICKS

LEVEL 2

Breadsticks are easy to make and these are especially delicious. They remind me of my in-laws: when my wife and I first started going out, her parents always served a ready supply of breadsticks before dinner. Unsurprisingly, they now love these. It feels good to be able to re-stock them with breadsticks; after all, I did run away with their daughter...

MAKES 40–50
Ingredients
500g strong white bread flour, plus more to dust
10g table salt
10g 'quick' yeast
2 tbsp dried rosemary (this seems a lot but, trust me, it works!)
200g pitted black olives in brine (drained weight)
250ml water
50ml olive oil

Tool Kit
rolling pin
tape measure
2 baking trays or sheets
2 wire cooling racks

1. Measure the flour, salt, yeast and rosemary into a bowl, making sure you add the salt and yeast to opposite sides of the bowl. Mix with a wooden spoon.

2. Finely chop the olives (leave nothing bigger than 5 x 5mm). Tip them into the bowl and mix in. Add the water and olive oil and mix with a wooden spoon until the flour has all come away from the bowl.

3. Tip out on to a floured work surface and knead for 5–10 minutes until smooth and elastic (the dough will turn a bit grey, due to the olives).

4. Roll out on a well-floured work surface into a rectangle about 50 x 25cm. Cut 40–50 strips out of the rectangle – widthways, so they are each 25cm long – and lay on 2 baking trays or sheets lined with baking parchment.

5. Cover with a plastic bag and leave for 20–30 minutes (the bag shouldn't touch the dough but should form a tent around it). Preheat the oven to 220°C/fan 200°C/gas 7.

6. Bake for 25–30 minutes. Take out and allow to cool completely on 2 wire racks to fully dry them out (this is important).

7. If they are not all hoovered up in a single sitting, store in an airtight container in a dry place and they will last for a few days before they turn soft.

Extras
Now you can make the dough, you can put whatever you like in it. My mum prefers green olives, so I always like to make an extra batch for her. Remember to cut the flavourings up quite small if you want to get straight sticks; any preserved vegetables, such as sun-dried tomatoes, work. Don't be afraid to chuck in the salt; it really helps the flavour. If you want your sticks to be harder, you can use wholemeal flour, and/or substitute 100g of your chosen flour with rye flour (although you'll need to add about 30ml water to the recipe as rye flour absorbs more). So, make these, knock up (or buy) a dollop of houmous and get stuck in. Be careful, though: once people get wind of them, you'll have to make loads more just to keep them satisfied.

GREEN OLIVE AND ROSEMARY FOCACCIA

One of my favourite breads for sharing. Whenever we have mates round at the weekend, I always make a few for dipping in oil and vinegar while we listen to the kids causing havoc in the garden. Focaccia has a good 'effort-to-glory' ratio too, so have a go and knock up a few loaves for yourself.

MAKES 2

Ingredients

500g strong white bread flour, plus more if needed

2 tsp table salt

1 tbsp 'quick' yeast

50ml olive oil, plus more to knead, prove and shape

350ml water

20 pitted green olives, in brine or oil

a few sprigs of rosemary

sea salt flakes and freshly coarse-ground black pepper

Tool Kit

empty ice-cream tub or large plastic container

2 baking trays

2 wire cooling racks

1. Measure the flour, salt and yeast into a bowl, making sure you add the salt and yeast to opposite sides of the bowl, then mix with a wooden spoon. Add the 50ml of olive oil and all the water and combine with the spoon until you have a wet dough.

2. Pour about 2 tbsp of olive oil on to a work surface and tip out the dough on to it. Knead for at least 10 minutes. The dough will be sloppy and this is going to be a messy business, so don't worry if you get your hands covered. Use your judgement about whether to add more flour; don't add too much, as it should remain a wet dough.

3. Oil an ice-cream tub or any large plastic container (more than 2-litre capacity) and plop the dough in. Cover with cling film and leave to rise at room temperature for 1–1½ hours until it has at least doubled in size. It might be worth taking a photo of the dough on your phone so you can compare later to see whether it has risen enough.

4. Pour another couple of tsp of oil on to a work surface and gently tip out the risen dough. Take 2 long knives and oil the blades. Cut the dough into 2 equal pieces: use 1 knife to cut them, then slide the other knife alongside the first and use both knives to push the halves apart. (This is the easiest way of prising the dough into 2 pieces.) Gently pick up each half and place on a baking tray lined with baking parchment, forming each into a thin lozenge shape.

5. Cover with a plastic bag and leave to rise for 45 minutes. (The bag shouldn't touch the loaves but should form a tent around them.)

6. Preheat the oven to 220°C/fan 200°C/gas 7 and uncover the dough. Cut the olives in half lengthways and press firmly into the dough. Drizzle with a few more tbsp of oil and lay cut sprigs of rosemary on top. Season with sea salt flakes and pepper.

7. Bake for 20–25 minutes, then remove and cool on 2 wire racks. Drizzle with more olive oil before cutting into strips and eating.

Extras

Try covering these with sun-dried tomatoes, marinated artichoke hearts or roast garlic cloves. Maybe stick a bit of Parma ham or grated Parmesan on top. Or use black olives instead of green. Just remember to make at least two loaves, because they are definitely for sharing.

BIG SOFT PRETZELS

For my wife's 30th birthday, we went to Oktoberfest in Munich to enjoy the rich culture, the beautiful buildings and the delicious food. We may have had a pint or two while we were there... Aside from a hangover, the main thing I brought back with me was a hankering for massive, soft, salty pretzels. After a few disasters, I reckon I've got them down. Have a go and see what you think.

MAKES 8

Ingredients

500g strong white bread flour, plus more to dust

50g light soft brown sugar

1 tbsp 'quick' yeast

2 tsp table salt

300ml warm water

a little flavourless oil, for the bowl

3 tbsp bicarbonate of soda

coarse sea salt or sea salt flakes, to sprinkle

Tool Kit

tape measure

pastry brush

baking tray

wire cooling rack

1. Measure the flour, sugar, yeast and salt into a bowl, making sure you add the salt and yeast to opposite sides of the bowl. Mix with a wooden spoon, then add the water and continue to mix, first with the spoon and then your hands, until all the flour has come away from the sides of the bowl.

2. Tip on to a lightly floured work surface and knead for 5–10 minutes until smooth and elastic.

3. Lightly oil the bowl, return the dough to it, cover with cling film and leave to rise at room temperature for 1–2 hours until at least doubled in size.

4. Tip out on to a floured surface and divide into 8 equal-sized pieces.

5. Roll each piece out into a thin 75cm-long worm. To make the classic pretzel shape, form the worm into an upside down 'U' in front of you. Take the 2 ends and twist them around each other twice, then press the end of the twists on to opposite sides of the 'U', sticking them on with a dab of water.

6. Preheat the oven to 240°C/fan 220°C/gas 9, and fill a large saucepan with 3.5 litres of boiling water. Add the bicarbonate of soda and line a baking tray with baking parchment. Using a slotted spoon, gently lower each pretzel into the boiling water and hold it there for 10 seconds, placing them on the prepared tray as you lift them out.

7. Slash the dough with a sharp knife, sprinkle with coarse sea salt, and bake for 15 minutes, or until a rich brown colour. Take out and allow to cool on a wire rack.

8. Try really hard not to eat them all in a single sitting.

Extras

These are great eaten still warm. The basic recipe works really well, but you can gussy it up with plenty of stuff:

Parmesan is great to sprinkle on with the coarse salt, as are sesame seeds, garlic salt or even piri piri seasoning.

You can make sweet pretzels: cinnamon sugar works well, as does drizzling the salted pretzels with icing or caramel after they're cooked. In fact, the salt-and-sweet combo is delicious.

CHALLAH ROLLS

LEVEL 3

Where I live in north London, challah is available from just about every bakery. It is a traditional Jewish bread, made from an enriched dough. On a Sunday morning, nothing beats a fresh challah roll with breakfast: it tastes flippin' fantastic! It can be made into a plaited loaf, but I like to make up a mass of dough, roll it out into loads of little sausages and shape rolls with my wife and kids. Everyone takes a turn and it's always fun seeing what our creations turn out like. Have a go at this; it's surprisingly easy to make.

MAKES 8–9
Ingredients
500g strong white bread flour,
    plus more to dust
1 tbsp 'quick' yeast
2 tsp table salt
45g caster sugar
2 tbsp poppy seeds, plus more
    to sprinkle
50ml vegetable oil, plus more
    for the bowl
2 tbsp runny honey
2 large eggs, lightly beaten,
    plus 1, also lightly
    beaten, to brush
170ml water

Tool Kit
tape measure
baking tray
pastry brush
wire cooling rack

1. Put the flour, yeast, salt, sugar and poppy seeds in a bowl, making sure you add the salt and yeast to opposite sides of the bowl, and mix together with a wooden spoon. Add the 50ml of oil, honey, the 2 eggs and the water and mix with the spoon until it has combined enough to handle, then keep mixing by hand until all the flour comes away from the sides of the bowl.

2. Tip out on to a lightly floured surface and knead for 5–10 minutes. Lightly oil the bowl and put the dough back in it. Cover with cling film and leave to rise at room temperature for 2–3 hours, or until doubled or tripled in size.

3. Tip out on to a lightly floured work surface once more and knead just to knock out the air.

4. To make each roll, take about 50g of dough and roll into a sausage about 30cm long; this forms the basis of each of the rolls you will be making. Make different shapes of roll (techniques shown overleaf). Once the rolls have been assembled, place them on a baking tray lined with baking parchment, leaving enough space between them for the dough to expand without the rolls sticking together.

5. Brush with the beaten egg, then sprinkle with poppy seeds. Cover with a plastic bag – the bag shouldn't touch the rolls but should form a tent around them – and leave to rise for 45 minutes. Meanwhile, preheat the oven to 200°C/fan 180°C/gas 6.

6. Bake the rolls for 15–20 minutes or until golden brown. Be sure to keep an eye on the colour towards the end of the bake, as enriched dough and egg wash can burn quite easily. If they start to look burnt, they'll be overdone.

7. Take out and cool on a rack; eat them all, then wish you had made double the quantity...

Extras
This dough is so versatile: you can make simple loaves or you can plait the dough using as many strands as your mind can cope with. You can use sesame seeds instead of poppy seeds. Apparently challah makes great toast, but I've never had enough left over to find out!

Below: making challah roll shapes

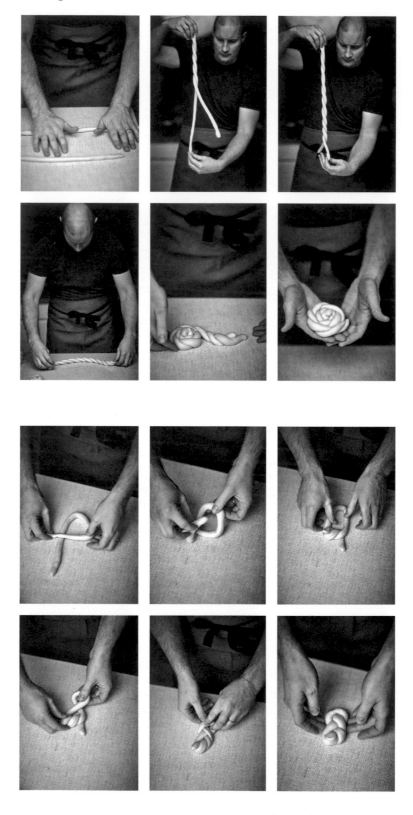

GOAT'S CHEESE, WALNUT AND PEAR PINWHEEL

STAR BAKE

Years ago, before our kids were born, we jumped into our tiny 1-litre motor and pootled off to France on a camping trip. We went to Sarlat in the Dordogne and spent a week wandering around markets and castles, drinking cheap wine and eating everything we could find. It was there that I developed a taste for the combination of goat's cheese and honey. This pinwheel tear-and-share reminds me of those days and of how we really need to go back with the kids, hide in a tent and bore them to sleep with tales of our youth.

MAKES 1
Ingredients

300g strong wholemeal
    bread flour
200g strong white bread flour,
    plus more to dust
25g pumpkin seeds
25g pine nuts
10g 'quick' yeast
10g table salt
300ml water
30ml olive oil, plus more for
    the bowl and to brush
4 Conference pears
1 egg, lightly beaten
75ml runny honey, plus more
    to serve
50g baby spinach leaves
150g goat's cheese, chopped
    into 1cm cubes
100g walnuts, chopped
sea salt flakes and freshly
    ground black pepper

Tool Kit

baking tray
rolling pin
your largest baking tray
    or sheet
pastry brush

1. Put the flours, seeds and pine nuts, yeast and salt in a bowl, making sure you add the salt and yeast on opposite sides, and mix with a wooden spoon. Add the water and the 30ml of olive oil. Mix by spoon and then by hand, until all the flour comes away from the sides.

2. Tip on to a lightly floured work surface and knead for 5–10 minutes, or until smooth and elastic. The seeds and nuts will keep falling out during the kneading, so keep poking them back in as you go.

3. Oil the bowl and put the dough back in, cover with cling film and set aside at room temperature for 1–1½ hours until doubled in size.

4. Meanwhile, preheat the oven to 160°C/fan 140°C/gas 3 and line a baking tray with baking parchment. Peel the pears, cut into quarters and cut out the cores, then slice 5mm thick. Lay the pear slices on the baking tray and put in the oven for 30 minutes to dry out (this will stop the bread from getting waterlogged with pear juice). Remove from the oven and set aside to cool.

5. Once the bread has risen, knead to knock back on a floured surface, divide into two and roll out each into a circle. The size is up to you, but don't make it bigger than your largest baking tray or sheet or you won't fit it in the oven (I normally make mine about 30cm in diameter). Lay out a large piece of baking parchment on the baking tray. Put one of the rolled-out discs of dough on the parchment.

6. Build the bread (see photographs overleaf). To start, paint a little of the beaten egg around the outside 2cm of the dough; this will be the 'glue' that sticks the top disc on. Remember not to put any filling on this outside edge. Drizzle honey on to the dough, avoiding the egg-washed edge. Be quite generous with this, as the sweetness will work well. Arrange a layer of spinach on top of the honey, then evenly cover with the goat's cheese, dried pears and walnuts. Roll the top disc of dough around a rolling pin and lay on top of the filled bottom layer, making sure to press down on to the egg-washed edges.

Continued...

7. Place a pint glass upside down in the middle and cut outwards from the glass into 16 segments, but don't chop through the baking parchment. Gently pick up each segment in turn, make two full twists and lay it down; be sure not to tear the dough. With scissors, snip a corner off each segment. Once all the segments are twisted, cover with baking parchment and leave to rise for 30 minutes.

8. Preheat the oven to 220°C/fan 200°C/gas 7 and uncover the dough; it should have risen. Lightly brush with a little olive oil and sprinkle with sea salt and pepper, but go easy with the salt as it is more flavoursome than table salt. Bake in the oven for 20–25 minutes or until golden brown, take out and drizzle with more honey. Eat!

Extras

Once you can make the basic pinwheel you can fill it with whatever you like. The open shape of the twists means that the fillings will cook through, so you can put in as much as you like without worrying.

2

SWEET DOUGH

BRIOCHE BURGER BUNS

For years I ate burgers in normal white bread buns. If I was feeling adventurous, I'd get those with a few sesame seeds sprinkled on them (woo hoo). But then I tried brioche buns and my life changed. Nothing compares to the sweet, buttery, absorbent, fluffy goodness of a brioche bun soaked in burger juice. Make these for your next barbecue and you'll never look back.

**MAKES 8 LARGE OR
12 MEDIUM BUNS**
Ingredients
400g strong white bread flour,
    plus more to dust
100g plain flour
2 tsp table salt
1 tbsp 'quick' yeast
60g caster sugar
125ml whole milk
4 large eggs, lightly beaten,
    plus 1, also lightly beaten,
    to brush
200g unsalted butter, at room
    temperature, cut into
    1cm cubes

Tool Kit
stand mixer fitted with dough
    hook (optional)
2 baking trays or sheets
pastry brush
wire cooling rack

1. Place the dry ingredients in the bowl of a stand mixer, or just in a bowl, putting the salt and yeast on opposite sides of the bowl. Mix in the milk and 4 eggs with a wooden spoon until everything is incorporated. You should get a sloppy, wet dough.

2. Knead, in a stand mixer fitted with a dough hook or by hand on a well-floured surface, adding the butter a few cubes at a time, for 10–15 minutes. It's messy, but persevere until the dough is stretchy.

3. Transfer the dough to a bowl, cover with cling film and leave at room temperature for 1–2 hours or until doubled or tripled in size.

4. Turn out on to a floured surface and knock back by folding the dough in on itself for a few minutes. Divide into 12 portions (if you want to be exact about it, weigh the dough and divide it by 12). Roll each piece up into a ball on a lightly floured surface and place the buns on 2 baking trays or sheets lined with baking parchment. The more you work this dough, the more the butter will melt in it from the heat of your hands, so don't hang about.

5. For the second prove, prop one tray on top of the other using herb jars as 'pillars'. Cover the trays with a plastic bag. You might want to prop up the top tray with herb jar pillars to stop the plastic from touching the dough; it should form a tent. Leave to rise for 2 hours.

6. Preheat the oven to 200°C/fan 180°C/gas 6 and take the bag off the trays. Brush each roll with egg and bake for 20–25 minutes or until golden brown. Now, this is enriched dough, so keep half an eye on the colour as the buns will burn easily.

7. Take out and cool on a wire rack, then cut in half and shove a really dirty burger in!

Extras
Brioche makes amazing bread and butter pudding, if it lasts that long.

Try mixing 100g of chocolate chips into the dough, or loading it with dried fruit. I'm not saying it'll change your life, but I reckon you'll be happier to be alive once you can make this. (Just don't eat these with burgers!)

These buns are especially good with my dad's burger salsa. Finely chop and mix together 500g vine tomatoes, ½ red onion, ½ cucumber, deseeded and peeled, a large bunch of coriander and 1 red chilli. Stir in 1 crushed garlic clove, 2 tsp caster sugar, 2 tbsp olive oil and 3 tbsp white wine vinegar and season with sea salt and freshly ground black pepper.

DOUBLE-GLAZED RING DOUGHNUTS

Mmmm, doughnuts... When I picture them, I channel Homer Simpson: cartoony ring doughnuts with pink icing and sprinkles. These are so easy to make and, once you've tried them, you'll never want shop-bought doughnuts again. A batch makes a great thank-you present in a box tied with ribbon.

MAKES ABOUT 12
Ingredients
For the doughnuts
150ml whole milk
50g unsalted butter
1 tbsp 'quick' yeast
20g caster sugar
330g strong white bread flour,
    plus more to dust
½ tsp table salt
1 large egg, lightly beaten
1.5 litres vegetable oil, to
    deep-fry, plus more for
    the baking trays

For the first glaze
100g icing sugar
3 tbsp boiling water

For the second glaze
50g fresh raspberries
150g icing sugar
50ml double cream
sprinkles/100s and 1,000s

Tool Kit
2 baking trays or sheets
rolling pin
9cm and 3cm round cutters
    (not essential, but useful)
deep-fat fryer (optional)
cooking thermometer
    (optional)
2 wire cooling racks
electric whisk (optional)

1. Place the milk in a small pan over a low heat to warm. Melt the butter in a separate pan over a low heat, then set aside. Mix the yeast with 1 tsp (5g) of the sugar and 50ml warm milk. Set aside for 15 minutes.

2. Sift the flour and the salt into a bowl. Stir in the remaining sugar. Pour in the yeast mix, remaining warm milk, melted butter and egg. Mix into a dough, knead for 5–10 minutes, then put into a bowl and cover with cling film. Leave to rise for 1 hour at room temperature.

3. Lightly oil 2 baking trays or sheets. Take the dough and knead on a floured work surface for a couple of minutes, just to knock it back. Roll it out to about 1cm thick and, with a 9cm round cutter (or a cardboard template and a sharp knife), cut out as many circles as you can. Using a small round cutter (around 3cm), punch out holes in the middles (or use an egg cup). Gently combine the offcuts and roll and cut out more circles until all the dough is used. Put the doughnuts on the prepared baking trays. Cover each with a plastic bag – the bag shouldn't touch the dough but should form a tent around it – and leave to rise again for about 45 minutes.

4. Heat the vegetable oil in a large saucepan (or deep-fat fryer) until it reaches 160°C. If you don't have a cooking thermometer, use a small piece of bread to see if it sizzles when dropped into the oil. Cook the doughnuts in batches, 3–4 at a time, for 1 minute each side, turning with a slotted spoon, until golden. Remove to cooling racks.

5. To make the first glaze, combine the icing sugar with the boiling water, mixing well to remove lumps. This next bit is messy so put kitchen paper under your cooling racks. Dip each doughnut in the glaze on both sides and leave to set on the cooling racks for 1 hour.

6. To make the second glaze, mush the raspberries through a sieve into a bowl. Add the icing sugar and mix well. Pour in the cream and whisk for about a minute with an electric whisk until it thickens up.

7. Pour the sprinkles onto a plate. Dip each doughnut into the icing, then the sprinkles. Leave on the racks to set for 1 hour, if you can wait.

Extras
Go mad with toppings: red for Valentine's Day; pastel for Easter. I like to use fruit in the glazes to give them more flavour, but you could use food colouring.

You can top them with edible glitter, gold or silver edible spray paint, anything you like... Let the littl'uns join in and decorate their own.

JAM DOUGHNUTS

One of my first jobs was washing up in a bakery. Every Saturday at 4.30am I'd drag my teenage self to work and get stuck in, cleaning everything in sight while gazing at the wonders being created around me. One of my favourite memories is of scrumping still-warm doughnuts as I carried them from the bakery to the shop. Don't be too hard on your friends if you find them sneakily stealing a few...

MAKES ABOUT 10
Ingredients
For the doughnuts
150ml whole milk
50g unsalted butter
1 tbsp 'quick' yeast
1½ tbsp caster sugar, plus
    about 150g more to coat
330g strong white bread flour,
    plus more to dust
¼ tsp table salt
1 large egg, lightly beaten
1.5 litres vegetable oil,
    to deep-fry, plus more
    for the baking trays

For the filling (optional)
200g fresh raspberries
150g caster sugar
1 tbsp lemon juice
OR use a standard-sized (340g)
    jar of shop-bought
    raspberry jam

Tool Kit
cooking thermometer
    (optional)
2 baking trays or sheets
deep-fat fryer (optional)
2 wire cooling racks
flavour injector

1. Place the milk in a small pan over a low heat to warm gently. Melt the butter in a separate pan over a low heat. Mix the yeast with ½ tbsp of the sugar and about 50ml of the warm milk. Set aside for 15 minutes.

2. Sift the flour and salt into a large bowl. Stir in the remaining 1 tbsp of sugar. Pour in the yeast mix, the rest of the warmed milk, the melted butter and egg. Mix into a dough, knead for 5–10 minutes, then put into a bowl and cover with cling film. Leave to rise for about 1 hour.

3. Meanwhile, if you're making the filling, put the raspberries, sugar and lemon juice in a saucepan. Stir over a low heat until all the sugar is dissolved, then increase the heat until the mixture is boiling. Keep stirring. Use a cooking thermometer and, when the jam reaches 105°C (or you can do the 'saucer test', see page 142), remove from the heat, transfer to a bowl and refrigerate.

4. When the doughnut dough has risen, knock it back for about a minute on a floured work surface. Divide into 10 equal-sized pieces (around 60g each) and roll each piece into a golf ball-sized ball. Oil 2 baking trays or sheets and lay the doughnuts on them. Cover each with a plastic carrier bag – the bag shouldn't touch the dough but should form a tent around it – and leave to rise again for about 45 minutes.

5. Heat the vegetable oil in a large saucepan (or in a deep-fat fryer) until it reaches 170°C. If you don't have a thermometer, drop in a small piece of white bread to see if it sizzles.

6. Use a slotted spoon to lower 3–4 doughnuts into the oil. Cook in batches for 30–60 seconds each side, turning with the slotted spoon, until lightly golden. Remove to cooling racks.

7. Load the flavour injector with raspberry jam. While the doughnuts are still warm, fill with jam by inserting the nozzle into the side of the doughnut, then roll each one in caster sugar to finish.

Extras
I like to use different-shaped cutters to make heart- and star-shaped doughnuts, by rolling the dough out to a 1cm thickness and punching out the shapes.

Try filling them with different jams, purées or flavoured custards.

Flavour the sugar to roll them in: try ginger, cinnamon or vanilla extract.

Glaze them with icing, or drizzle them with caramel (see overleaf) or chocolate.

APPLE AND CINNAMON CHELSEA BUNS

LEVEL 2

I have two apple trees in my garden and, from late summer onwards, I have cooking apples coming out of my ears. No matter how much I cook with them – in apple pies, tarts and sauce, baked, stewed – they still keep coming! This is a great batch-bake to share with workmates or to make for a bake sale. If you have an autumn morning to spare, making these is an ideal way to spend it.

MAKES 15 (18 IF YOU ROLL IT OUT FAR ENOUGH)

Ingredients

For the buns

500g strong white bread flour, plus more to dust
7g table salt
7g 'quick' yeast
50g unsalted butter, plus more for the tin
250ml whole milk
1 large egg
1 large cooking apple
100g caster sugar
1 tbsp ground cinnamon
100g raisins
50g flaked almonds

For the caramel topping

100g caster sugar
35g unsalted butter, chopped into 1cm cubes
50ml double cream

Tool Kit

rolling pin
tape measure
pastry brush
large roasting tin (preferably about 40 x 30cm)
2 wire cooling racks
piping bag (optional)

1. Mix the flour, salt and yeast in a bowl, making sure you put the salt and yeast on opposite sides of the bowl before mixing. Melt the butter in a small saucepan over a gentle heat. Slightly warm the milk in a separate pan, pour it into a jug and beat in the egg and butter, then pour all the wet ingredients into the bowl with the flour. Mix well, with a wooden spoon first and then your fingers, until you have a rough dough. Turn out on to a floured work surface and knead for 5–10 minutes until a smooth dough is formed. Put the dough in a bowl, cover with cling film and leave for 1–1½ hours at room temperature until it has at least doubled in size.

2. Meanwhile, prepare the filling by peeling and coring the apple and chopping it finely. Lay it on a sheet of kitchen paper on a chopping board. Lay some more kitchen paper over it, put another chopping board on top and put a heavy book on top of that to help press out some of the juice. Mix the sugar with the cinnamon and set aside in a bowl.

3. Clear a big area to roll out on – you need at least 80 x 40cm – and flour it well. Tip out the dough on to the surface and begin to roll out into a rectangle at least 60 x 40cm. You may need to let the dough rest every now and again to allow it to stretch to the full size, but remember to keep the underside well floured, or it will stick.

4. Once the rectangle is made, evenly sprinkle the sugar/cinnamon mix on to the dough, but try to keep the 4–5cm edge of dough closest to you clear. Once this is done, evenly sprinkle the chopped apple, raisins and flaked almonds on to the dough, remembering to keep the long edge closest to you clear.

5. Now roll it up. Start with the long edge furthest away from you and gently roll it towards you. This will feel fiddly at first, but will get easier as the roll gets thicker. When the roll is almost done, brush the clear strip of dough with water and finish the rolling, so the water sticks the roll closed. You should now have a long sausage of dough. If you want it longer, you can gently stretch it by lifting it off the surface and pulling it out. Be gentle! You don't want to rip it.

6. Get a large roasting tin, preferably about 40 x 30cm, and butter it lightly. Using a sharp knife, cut the dough in lengths of 4–5cm.

Continued...

Gently put each in the roasting tin, cut side up, leaving a 1cm gap between each to allow the buns to expand. Cover with cling film, and leave to rise somewhere warm for about 1 hour.

7. Meanwhile, make the caramel. Put the sugar in a pan with 4 tbsp of water and heat until the sugar has melted and turned golden brown. (If it turns dark brown, it's burnt, and you have to start again!) Once golden brown, reduce the heat and add the butter, stirring all the while. Be careful, because this will bubble up. After about 1 minute of stirring, pour in the cream and continue to stir. Once the cream is mixed in, pour into a heatproof bowl and set aside to cool.

8. Preheat the oven to 200°C/fan 180°C/gas 6, take the cling film off the roasting tin and bake the buns for 25 minutes or until golden brown. Take out, set on wire racks and allow to cool. Drizzle the caramel over the buns with a spoon, or use a piping bag if you have one.

Extras
This recipe is delicious as it is, but you can muck about with it in any way you choose.

It's a great way of using up any leftovers lurking at the back of the kitchen cupboards, such as nuts (make sure they're not rancid!) and dried fruit.

You can turn the topping into salted caramel by adding ½ tsp of table salt when you add the cream.

Or top them with glacé icing.

Personally, I love savoury Chelsea buns, too: try green or red pesto, or tomato passata, both lovely to spread on. Roasted vegetables, bacon bits, olives, grated cheese, even leftovers from Sunday lunch can taste great! Have fun with them.

PANETTONE

My wife Sarah has Italian heritage, so for the past 14 years I've been the lucky guy who gets to scoff his way through loads of panettone each Christmas. This light, delicious bread is just brilliant dipped in dessert wine. I've put chocolate in my version, which isn't traditional, but hey, it's my book and if I want to fill everything with chocolate, then that's what I'm going to do. From the moment I begin zesting the oranges for this, I'm always filled with a desperate urge to start eating. It's a wonder I'm never caught scoffing the raw dough. The most important thing to remember with this bread is *patience*. Give it as much time as it needs to rise.

MAKES 1 LARGE PANETTONE
Ingredients

50g currants
50g sultanas
100g candied mixed peel
finely grated zest of 1 orange
    and 1 unwaxed lemon
1 tbsp dark rum
120ml whole milk
150g caster sugar
1 tbsp 'quick' yeast
500g strong white bread flour
1 tsp table salt
180g unsalted butter, cut into
    1cm cubes, plus more for
    the tin
3 large eggs, lightly beaten,
    plus 1, also lightly beaten,
    to brush
1 tsp vanilla bean paste
50g chocolate chips
a little flavourless oil, for
    the bowl

Tool Kit

stand mixer fitted with dough
    hook (optional)
panettone tin, or 23cm (or
    wider) deep-sided
    springform cake tin
pastry brush
wire cooling rack

1. Put the currants, sultanas and candied peel into a bowl with the zests and the rum, cover with cling film and leave to soak for 20 minutes.

2. Put 60ml of the milk and 10g of the caster sugar in a bowl and microwave for 15 seconds on full power (or heat gently in a small saucepan). Stir this up, then stir in the yeast. Leave to stand for 15 minutes, until it becomes frothy.

3. Tip the flour, remaining sugar and the salt into the bowl of a stand mixer and mix well, then stir in the butter. Add the yeast mixture, remaining milk, 3 eggs, vanilla bean paste, chocolate chips and soaked fruit and mix up thoroughly using a silicone spatula.

4. Fit the stand mixer with a dough hook, turn it on to a medium speed and knead for 10 minutes. This is going to be a wet dough – almost cakey in consistency due to the huge amount of butter in it – but don't worry!

5. Transfer the dough to an oiled bowl, cover with cling film and leave to rise at room temperature for 2–3 hours or until at least doubled in size (tripled is better; take a photo on your phone for comparison purposes).

6. Rub some butter on the inside of a panettone tin, or a 23cm (or wider) deep-sided springform tin, and use the sticky surface to line it with baking parchment. Knock back the risen dough and put it in the prepared tin. Cover the tin with a plastic bag, to form a tent around it, and leave to rise for another 2–3 hours, or until the dough has risen to at least 2cm above the rim of the tin.

7. Preheat the oven to 200°C/fan 180°C/gas 6 and brush the top of the panettone with the remaining egg.

8. Bake for 40–45 minutes, checking during the last 15 minutes to see if the top is browning too much. If it is, cover it with foil for the rest of the bake. Take out and leave to cool on a wire rack.

Extras

Now, in terms of changing the constituent parts of panettone, I'd avoid it if I were you. The large amounts of eggs, milk and butter in the mix means that the yeast works very slowly, hence the long proving times involved.

CHEEKY MONKEY BREAD

Doughnuts are all well and good, but what if you absolutely must have a mountain of them all stuck together with caramel? Look no further, because all your doughnut mountain problems are solved here. Monkey bread is a really good centrepiece dessert, especially if you have kids and don't mind them getting incredibly messy while they tear off the bits. This sticky cinnamon version is great with a big blob of ice cream, but for me it's the caramel sauce that makes it so addictive.

MAKES 1 LARGE TEAR-AND-SHARE 'LOAF'

Ingredients

For the dough

500g strong white bread flour, plus more to dust

2 tsp table salt

3 tbsp caster sugar

1 tbsp 'quick' yeast

100g unsalted butter, cut into 1cm cubes, plus more for the tin

2 large eggs, lightly beaten

200ml whole milk

For the coating

100g unsalted butter

150g light soft brown sugar

1 tbsp ground cinnamon

For the caramel sauce

150g unsalted butter

150g light soft brown sugar

1 tsp vanilla bean paste

Tool Kit

Bundt tin

serving plate

1. Tip the flour, salt, sugar and yeast into a bowl, making sure you put the salt and the yeast on opposite sides of the bowl, then mix with a wooden spoon. Add the butter, eggs and milk. Mix until combined enough to handle, then tip out on to a well-floured work surface.

2. Knead for 5–10 minutes, until the dough becomes smooth and elastic. This dough will be quite sticky at first, but will come good as the cubes of butter are incorporated. If you need to add more flour to stop it sticking, be careful not to go mad or it will dry out the dough.

3. Put the dough in a bowl, cover with cling film and leave to rise at room temperature for 1–1½ hours, or until at least doubled in size.

4. Thoroughly butter a Bundt tin. To start the coating, melt the butter in a small saucepan over a low heat. Mix the sugar and cinnamon in a bowl.

5. Tip out the risen dough on to a floured surface and knock back by folding the dough in on itself for a minute or so. Divide into around 40 small balls. Dip each dough ball into the melted butter, roll it in the cinnamon sugar, then pop it into the prepared tin.

6. Once all the dough is used up, cover the tin with a plastic bag and leave to rise for about 1 hour.

7. Preheat the oven to 200°C/fan 180°C/gas 6. Make the caramel sauce by melting the butter in a pan, then stirring in the sugar and vanilla bean paste until the sugar has dissolved. Pour the melted mixture over the risen dough, then bake for 30 minutes.

8. Take out of the oven and leave to cool, with the tin upside down, on a plate. After 5 minutes, take the tin off, put the bread in the middle of the dinner table and tear, share and eat with ice cream.

Extras

I've yet to find something sweet that I wouldn't want to tip on a pile of monkey bread, but a few of my favourite things are maple syrup, golden syrup, melted chocolate and salted caramel (yum). You can also cover it with crushed nuts, raspberries, blueberries or whipped cream. Sometimes it's nice to add walnut or pecan halves and chopped sticky dried figs while filling the tin, so they get baked into the bread itself. And since it is called monkey bread, try adding chopped-up banana and drizzling with golden syrup... lovely!

SWEDISH WREATH

This always looks impressive and I find it great fun to make. It's a good one if you want to show off, as rolling out the dough into a massive sheet and sprinkling over the filling can be a real spectacle. This is a bake that can use up all of those half-bags of dried fruit in your cupboards, which I find really useful to do now and again. If you're having friends over for tea, this certainly brightens things up… just no fighting over the last slice, please.

MAKES 1 LARGE LOAF
Ingredients
For the wreath

430g strong white bread flour, plus more to dust

7g table salt

10g 'quick' yeast

125g caster sugar

25g unsalted butter, chopped into 1cm cubes, plus more for the bowl

2 large eggs, lightly beaten

80ml whole milk

100ml water

75g dried apple

3 tsp ground cinnamon

75g candied mixed peel

75g sultanas

For the toppings

100g apricot jam

100g icing sugar

1 tbsp lemon juice

50g pecans

Tool Kit

rolling pin

tape measure

pastry brush

baking tray

wire cooling rack

piping bag

1. Put the flour in a bowl and add the salt and yeast to different sides. Tip in 25g of the sugar and mix with a wooden spoon, then stir in the butter. Add the eggs to the milk with the water, then pour this into the bowl. Mix with the spoon until combined enough to mix with your hands, then tip on to a well-floured work surface and knead for 5–10 minutes until the dough is smooth and stretchy.

2. Put the dough into a lightly buttered bowl, cover with cling film and leave somewhere warm for 1 hour, until doubled or tripled in size.

3. Cut the dried apple up with scissors into pieces about the same size as the sultanas. Mix the cinnamon with the remaining 100g of sugar.

4. Once the dough has risen, tip it out on to a lightly floured surface and knock back by gently folding in on itself for about a minute. Roll the dough out into a rectangle about 60 x 40cm, in landscape orientation as you look at it. The dough will still be a bit tight after the knocking back, so you may need to rest it for 5 minutes. Try to make sure the corners are as sharp as you can get.

5. Once the dough is rolled out evenly, sprinkle the cinnamon sugar over, making sure not to cover the 5cm edge closest to you as this is the bit that will stick the ring together later. Evenly sprinkle all the dried fruit over the dough and brush the bare edge closest to you with water. Now roll it up. Start with the long edge furthest away from you and gently roll it towards you. Use the wetted edge to stick the roll closed. Leave it for 5 minutes to stick well. (See photographs on pages 46–7.)

6. Line a baking tray with baking parchment. Curl the rolled dough into a ring. The ends of the ring will probably be a bit messy, so use a very sharp knife to cut ragged edges off and stick the ends together with a bit of water. Try to keep the seam of the ring underneath and out of sight. Transfer the newly formed ring on to the prepared baking tray.

7. Using a large pair of scissors, cut into the ring, going about two-thirds of the way in with each cut, at intervals every 3–4cm (see photographs on page 47). Gently stretch out each segment and twist it about 45 degrees to expose the fruit swirls inside. Place a plastic bag over the baking tray to form a tent and leave to rise for 1 hour.

Continued…

8. Preheat the oven to 220°C/fan 200°C/gas 7 and bake for 25 minutes, keeping an eye on the ring during the last 10 minutes to make sure it doesn't burn. If it does begin to colour too much, cover with foil.

9. Meanwhile, put the jam into a saucepan with 1 tbsp of water and place over a low heat. Once the ring is cooked, take it out of the oven and set on a cooling rack. Paint the hot jam on to the still warm ring; use plenty!

10. Make the icing by beating the icing sugar and lemon juice together. Once smooth, transfer to a piping bag and pipe on to the cooled ring. Use the icing to stick pecans on to the ring to decorate, then serve.

Extras

This is something I often bake after Christmas, when I've got loads of extra ingredients lying around the kitchen. In fact, I like to put a bit of marzipan in mine too and, this year, I even tried one with a jar of mincemeat in it (it was delicious, if a bit sticky!). Definitely have a go at this bake; it looks a treat and – once you've mastered transferring the ring on to the baking tray – the rest is plain sailing.

3

CAKES

VICTORIA SPONGE

You can totally make this cake! It is so easy that it is the only recipe in this book for which I'm putting in almost no measurements. Once you've got the hang of making this, the world of cake will open up for you. For me, this was the gateway cake that got me hooked on baking many years ago. Hopefully it'll do the same for you. It's important that everything is at room temperature, so if your butter is chilly, chop it into 2cm blocks, put it into a jug of tepid water for 10 minutes to soften it up, then drain.

MAKES 1 | SERVES 8–10
Ingredients
unsalted butter (the same
    weight as the eggs), at
    room temperature, plus
    more for the tins
4 large eggs
caster sugar (the same weight
    as the eggs)
plain flour (the same weight
    as the eggs)
1 tsp baking powder
1 tsp vanilla bean paste
100g strawberry jam
300ml double cream
a little icing sugar, to dust

Tool Kit
2 x 20cm round sandwich tins
electric whisk
wire cooling rack

1. Preheat the oven to 200°C/fan 180°C/gas 6 and butter 2 x 20cm round sandwich tins. Butter the tins and line with baking parchment. Preheat the oven to 180°C/fan 160°C/gas 4.

2. Put a bowl on to your kitchen scales and set the weight to zero. Crack the eggs into the bowl, write down the weight, then set them aside. Weigh out the butter and put it into a large mixing bowl with the equal weight of sugar. Beat together with an electric whisk until the colour lightens and the texture goes smooth. Weigh out the flour in a separate bowl and mix the baking powder into it.

3. A little at a time, thoroughly beat the eggs into the butter mixture with the vanilla bean paste. If the mixture starts to split, add 1 tbsp of the flour. Sift the remaining flour into the mixing bowl and gently fold the batter together by cutting through the middle of the mixture with a spatula, turning it over, then rotating the bowl slightly and repeating until fully combined. Be careful not to over-mix; you don't want to knock too much air out of your batter.

4. Divide the batter equally between the prepared tins, spreading it out smoothly. Bake for 20–25 minutes, or until a cocktail stick comes out clean when poked into the centre. For the first 20 minutes of baking, do not open the oven door, or your cake will sink. Take out and leave on a cooling rack until cold.

5. Tip the jam into a bowl and mix up with a spoon to loosen. In a separate bowl, whisk the cream with an electric whisk until it forms soft peaks.

6. Spread the jam on to the bottom (least attractive) sponge, then spread the cream over and put on the top (most attractive) sponge. Dust with icing sugar and serve.

Extras
As long as you get the ingredient weights right – and get the hang of checking to see if the sponge is cooked – you can nail this cake every time. Throughout my life it has been a constant fixture, whether at teatime with family and friends, or as a base for countless birthday cakes. It may be humble, but it's classic and always welcome at my table.

CHOCOLATE CAKE

Everyone needs a go-to chocolate cake and this is mine. It's easy to make, pretty speedy and very delicious. If you're in a bind and need to knock up a cake quick-smart, have a crack at this; it requires minimal shopping and provides maximum glory.

MAKES 1 | SERVES 8–10
Ingredients
For the cake
200g unsalted butter, softened, plus more for the tins
125g dark chocolate (70 per cent cocoa solids)
2 tsp instant coffee
200g caster sugar
4 large eggs
200g plain flour
50g cocoa powder
1½ tsp baking powder

For the ganache and topping
500g dark chocolate (70 per cent cocoa solids)
500ml double cream
fresh raspberries (optional)

Tool Kit
2 x 20cm round sandwich tins
electric whisk
wire cooling rack
cake-cutting wire (optional)
offset palette knife

1. Preheat the oven to 180°C/fan 160°C/gas 4. Cut baking parchment discs for the bases of 2 x 20cm round sandwich tins. Butter the tins and lay the papers in.

2. Break the dark chocolate into a heatproof bowl and set over a saucepan of water on a medium-low heat (the bowl should not touch the water). Once melted, set aside until cool, but not set. Mix the coffee with 3 tbsp of boiling water and set aside to cool.

3. Put the butter and sugar into a bowl and beat with an electric whisk until light and creamy. Thoroughly beat in each egg, one by one. If the mixture starts to split, add 1 tbsp of the flour to bring it back.

4. Sift in the rest of the flour, the cocoa powder and baking powder, then fold them in. Be gentle, but make sure the mixture is fully combined, including any flour at the bottom of the bowl. Pour in the melted chocolate and the coffee and fold in. Divide the batter between the prepared tins, smooth it out and bake for 18–20 minutes.

5. Meanwhile, make the ganache by breaking the chocolate into a heatproof bowl. Put the cream in a saucepan and bring to the boil. As soon as it's boiling, tip it into the chocolate and mix. Leave to cool.

6. Check that each cake is cooked by poking a cocktail stick into the centre: if it comes out clean then it's cooked; if it's got cake mix on it, give the cake another 2 minutes before testing again. Take out and set on a wire rack. Once cool enough to touch, pop the cakes out of the tins and return to the rack to fully cool.

7. Cut each cake in half, either by using a cake-cutting wire or a long serrated knife. Save the prettiest layer for the top and set the bottom layer on a plate or cake board. Spread a layer of ganache on the bottom layer, then gently press the next layer on. Build the rest of the layers up, then cover the entire cake with the remaining ganache using a palette knife. Add the raspberries to the top of the cake, if you want. Leave the ganache to set, then eat.

Extras
You can use this basic recipe to build chocolate structures and multi-layered cakes. I like to cover the top in raspberries – the sharpness balances the rich chocolate – but top it with whatever you like; try sprinkles, or other fruits.

Cover the cake with the simple ganache in this recipe, or chocolate buttercream.

You can up the coffee content to 5 tsp, stick some chocolate-covered coffee beans on top and make it into a mocha cake.

JAMAICAN GINGER CAKE

LEVEL 1

Who doesn't remember opening a silver-lined packet of dark, sticky Jamaican ginger cake? When I was a kid, one of my favourite treats was scraping the leftover cake off the packaging and scoffing it from the knife... happy days. Now I've amplified that experience by making my whole house smell of molasses and ginger while my version of the cake is baking. This is great, easy, but requires self-control, as it tastes a lot better if it has a day to mature after being cooked. The smell may be torture, but you'll be well rewarded for your patience.

SERVES 10
Ingredients

160g unsalted butter, softened,
    plus more for the tin
100g black treacle
160g dark soft brown sugar
250g plain flour
1 tbsp ground ginger
1 tsp ground cinnamon
1 tsp freshly grated nutmeg
1 tsp bicarbonate of soda
200ml whole milk
1 large egg, lightly beaten
50g crystallised ginger,
    finely chopped

Tool Kit

900g loaf tin or 23cm round,
    deep-sided cake tin
electric whisk
wire cooling rack

1. Preheat the oven to 190°C/fan 170°C/gas 5. Line a 900g loaf tin or a 23cm round, deep cake tin by rubbing butter on to the tin, then sticking baking parchment to the inside.

2. Measure the black treacle into a mixing bowl. Add the brown sugar and softened butter and beat with an electric whisk until light(ish) and fluffy.

3. In a separate bowl, sift together the flour, spices and bicarb.

4. Add half the milk to the treacle mixture and beat together. Now this will split a bit, so add about one-quarter of the dry ingredients to counteract the splitting, and beat together. Beat in the remaining milk, the egg, then the remaining dry ingredients and the crystallised ginger, making sure to incorporate all the flour. Pour the batter into the prepared tin and spread out until smooth and even.

5. Bake for 55–65 minutes or until a skewer poked into the centre comes out clean. Remove from the oven and let stand for 5 minutes before taking the cake out of the tin and allowing to cool on a wire rack.

6. Once fully cooled, wrap up in foil and allow the cake to mature for a day or so. This will make it sticky and rich: it's well worth it!

Extras

My mum always tells me to add more ginger. Not just to this, but to everything I make with ginger in it, so feel free to double or even triple the crystallised ginger in this recipe. You can even add 1–2 tbsp grated root ginger if you like the zing it gives.

I can't stress enough the importance of letting this cake sit for a day or so. You can even do a taste test if you're really impatient, so you can see for yourself. The spices I have put in are a combination I like, but the Jamaican ginger police won't arrest you if you want to muck about with different ingredients, so go for it. Just remember: there is a lot of strong flavour in this cake, so putting weedy flavours in will probably have little effect.

Have fun messing around with it... or rigidly stick to my recipe. Either way you can't beat it as an accompaniment to a sit down and a cuppa.

CHERRY AND ALMOND SWISS ROLL

LEVEL 2

A lot of people baulk at Swiss rolls but, I promise you, they are easier to make than they look. They are such a simple treat and can be made in so many ways… you could dedicate a whole book just to rolling up cake. Because they are made in a sheet they take the shortest time to cook, which means – if you're not putting cream in them – they are a really quick treat. This one takes a little longer, but only so I can show you how to jazz it up by freezing decorations into it.

MAKES 1 | SERVES 6–8

Ingredients

For the filling

150g ripe cherries

150g jam sugar

1 tbsp lemon juice

300ml double cream

For the sponge

unsalted butter, for the tin

3 large eggs, separated

75g caster sugar, plus more
  to sprinkle

½ tsp almond extract

50g plain flour

red gel food colour

50g ground almonds

Tool Kit

Swiss roll tin (about 33 x 23cm)

electric whisk

small piping bag

2 wire cooling racks

1. Start by making the filling. Stone the cherries, cut each into eighths and put in a pan with the jam sugar and lemon juice. Cook over a medium heat until boiling, then reduce the heat and continue to cook for a further 15 minutes. Take off the heat, pour into a bowl and, once it's at room temperature, put in the fridge to chill.

2. To make a pattern on the Swiss roll, first of all check that you can fit a Swiss roll tin, about 33 x 23cm, into your freezer. Cut a piece of baking parchment to the size of the tin and draw on your pattern in pencil. I recommend starting with stripes or spots. For stripes, draw diagonal lines on to the paper about 5cm apart.

3. Butter the Swiss roll tin, then line the base with the baking parchment, pencil side down.

4. To make the sponge, beat the egg yolks with 30g of the sugar and the almond extract, using an electric whisk. Clean your beaters thoroughly and, in a separate bowl, use the whisk to beat the egg whites with the remaining sugar until firm peaks form. Sift the flour into the yolk mixture, then gently fold it in with the egg whites until fully combined. Try to be gentle, you don't want to lose too much of the air that you've beaten into the egg.

5. Take 3 tbsp of the mixture and put into a separate bowl. Gently mix with some red gel food colour until a rich red colour has formed. (Gel colours are much better than liquid, as they add less moisture but also more colour.) Load the coloured mixture into a piping bag, cut a very small hole in the tip, then pipe stripes on to your template in the tin. Put into the freezer for 15–20 minutes to harden.

6. Preheat the oven to 190°C/fan 170°C/gas 5 and fold the ground almonds into the remaining cake mixture with a spatula. Take the Swiss roll tin out of the freezer and pour the almond sponge mixture on, gently spreading out with a spatula or a palette knife, and quickly put in the oven before the frozen mix melts and spreads. Cook for 8–9 minutes until the top of the sponge is just coloured. Take out and rest on a wire rack in its tin for 5 minutes, but no longer or the sponge will dry out.

7. Sprinkle a fine layer of caster sugar on to a sheet of baking parchment on a second cooling rack and turn the sponge out of the tin and on to this (see left). The sugar will stop the sponge from

Continued…

sticking to the parchment. Gently peel the backing off the sponge; the pattern will be facing upwards. Put another sugared piece of baking parchment on to the first cooling rack and flip the sponge back over so the pattern is facing down. Using a serrated knife, score a line 2cm in along one of the short edges, about half the depth of the sponge. Starting from the scored edge, roll the sponge up, along with the baking parchment it is resting on, into a fairly tight roll. Leave on a wire rack to finish cooling (about 20 minutes).

8. Whisk the cream with the electric whisk until it forms soft peaks. Unroll the sponge and spread the cold cherry jam on the top. Evenly spread the cream on top of the jam and roll back up. The red pattern on the outside of the sponge should look quite vivid and the roll should be quite tight, with no open spaces and not sagging. Serve on a plate and eat quickly (before anyone else does).

Extras

This basic recipe will make a very delicious Bakewell-flavoured Swiss roll, with cherry-coloured stripes on the outside. Now that you can roll up a sponge and layer colours on to it, you can make some really beautiful designs. If you feel like making multiple colours, you can; just remember to freeze between each colour. If you want to try writing words on to the Swiss roll, such as 'Will You Marry Me?' (invite me to the wedding if you actually do this), then write in pencil on the baking parchment, but make sure you turn the paper and put it in the tin pencil side down so that you pipe the words 'backwards'.

For this recipe, I've made almond sponge, but you can make any flavour you want, just replace the ground almonds with other ground nuts, or more plain flour, and you're good to go. If you want to make a plain sponge, stick in ½ tsp vanilla bean paste; it makes all the difference.

I've filled this with jam and cream, but use lemon curd (see page 142) or crème pâtissière (see page 61) to add another dimension. Just don't over-fill the roll or you won't be able to roll it back up again; 200–250g will be enough.

There, that's loads of things to muck about with, so have fun and make some really pretty and delicious cakes.

MINCEMEAT CUPCAKES

LEVEL 2

My mum makes a mincemeat cake every year without fail. I'm not sure where she got her recipe, but she has perfected it over the years, and now I'm going to stick it in a book. It is delicious and makes the week after New Year something to look forward to (in cake terms, anyway), as all the mincemeat is half-price. I've played around with it to make really light cupcakes with brandy butter cream. I'm not really a cupcake person, but I think these are the best I've tasted. If you've still got the Christmas bug in January – or if you find mince pies a bit heavy – make these and I promise you'll agree! This is a level 2 recipe because – though the cakes are pretty simple – piping buttercream is a skill to master.

MAKES 12
Ingredients
For the cupcakes
60g unsalted butter, softened
100g caster sugar
1 large egg, lightly beaten
125ml whole milk
410g mincemeat (about 1 regular jar, or see page 142 for home-made)
200g plain flour
3 tsp baking powder

For the buttercream
150g unsalted butter, softened
300g icing sugar
2 tbsp brandy

Tool Kit
electric whisk
12 large cupcake or muffin cases
12-hole muffin tin
wire cooling rack
piping bag
large star-tipped nozzle

1. Preheat the oven to 180°C/fan 160°C/gas 4.

2. Beat the butter and sugar together with an electric whisk until light coloured and smooth. Thoroughly beat in the egg, then stir in the milk; the mixture will split here, but don't worry – it will come back when you put the flour in. Stir in the mincemeat to get a really sloppy-looking mixture.

3. Sift the flour and baking powder together and fold into the batter. This will make quite a wet mixture, but trust me, it'll turn out fine!

4. Place the cases in a muffin tin and load each with 2 heaped tbsp of batter; this should use it all up. Bake for 20 minutes, or until a cocktail stick comes out clean when stuck in the centre of a cake.

5. Once cooked, remove from the oven, take the cakes out of the muffin tin and set on a wire rack to cool. They must be fully cooled before the buttercream can go on, or it will melt.

6. Make the buttercream by beating the butter, icing sugar and brandy in a bowl with the electric whisk until fully combined and creamy.

7. Load the buttercream into a piping bag fitted with a large star-tipped nozzle, but do not put it in the fridge if you're not piping the cupcakes straight away or it will stiffen up too much to pipe. Pipe swirls of buttercream on to each cake: start on the outside and spiral your way in, leaving a point in the middle. Eat!

Extras

One of the things I love most about this recipe is the rich, fruity taste you get for relatively little effort. Feel free to make your own mincemeat and incorporate it into this cake, but I secretly enjoy the thrill of picking up mincemeat cheap in January and making something really delicious out of it. You can make this into a big cake, too, if you put the batter in a lined, buttered 23cm tin and bake for 30–40 minutes; my mum likes to sprinkle flaked almonds on it before baking, which tastes great. As long as you check with a cocktail stick that it's done, you'll turn out delicious cakes every time.

PINEAPPLE UPSIDE-DOWN CAKE

There's a fantastic South American barbecue restaurant near where I live. You sit at the table and they relentlessly pile different meats on to your plate until you can't take it any more and press a red button on the table to make them stop! At that point, they come around with barbecued pineapple and – even though you're bursting at the seams – no one can resist sweet, caramelised pineapple slices. This cake is my nod to that. If you feel like evoking the 1970s for pudding one evening, you can do a lot worse than having a crack at this. It is a bit old-fashioned, but I dare you to try not to reach for another slice once you've had a taste.

MAKES 1 | SERVES 8–10
Ingredients
110g unsalted butter, at room
    temperature, plus more for
    the tin
155g caster sugar
1 can (about 420g) of pineapple
    slices in juice
75g glacé cherries
2 large eggs
50g ground almonds
100g plain flour
1 tsp baking powder
½ tsp ground ginger
½ tsp mixed spice

Tool Kit
23cm round sandwich tin
    (not loose-bottomed)
electric whisk
wire cooling rack
serving plate

1. Butter a 23cm round sandwich tin and evenly scatter in 30g (2 tbsp) of the sugar.

2. Drain the pineapple slices. Put the first ring into the centre of the tin. Cut the remaining slices in half and arrange the crescents around the centre ring like a fan; there should be room for about 12 halves. Place cherries in the ring holes, including in the centre.

3. Preheat the oven to 200°C/fan 180°C/gas 6. Beat the butter and remaining sugar together until fluffy, using an electric whisk. Add the eggs, one by one, beating thoroughly each time, then beat in the ground almonds. You'll need to scrape down the sides of your bowl, to fully mix all the wet ingredients.

4. In a separate bowl, sift together the flour, baking powder and spices.

5. Fold the dry ingredients into the wet mixture using a silicone spatula, making sure not to leave any unmixed flour at the bottom.

6. Pour the cake batter over the pineapple slices and bake for 30–35 minutes, or until a cocktail stick comes out clean when prodded into the centre of the cake.

7. Take out of the oven and leave to cool for 5 minutes on a wire rack, then put your serving plate face down on top of the sandwich tin and turn the whole thing upside down to get the cake out of the tin (you may need to prise a pineapple slice gently from the bottom and replace it on the cake). Serve with coconut ice cream.

Extras
Upside-down cakes work with any soft fruit you can get out of the garden, or even with apples. Fruits such as blackberries, blackcurrants, blueberries and raspberries all work well with apple. The cooking time is usually the same no matter what fruit you put in and they really taste and look ace, so get to it.

FRAISIER CAKE

LEVEL 3

This has been a favourite of mine for years, as it makes such a striking centrepiece. I love a strawberry-pistachio combo, too. Although we're in level 3 territory, don't be afraid to have a crack at it. Nothing here is especially complicated; in fact, a lot of the time is spent waiting for things to cool, so you can get on with something else. So no excuses: if you see some nice strawberries when you're out, get them and make a fraisier; the 'effort-to-awesomeness' ratio is certainly in your favour if you do.

MAKES 1 | SERVES 10–12

Ingredients

For the crème pâtissière

300ml whole milk

1 tsp vanilla extract

3 large egg yolks (save 1 of the whites in a cup, and 2 in another cup)

25g cornflour

50g caster sugar

25g unsalted butter

150ml double cream

For the pistachio syrup

30g pistachios

50g caster sugar

For the pistachio sponge

4 large eggs

150g caster sugar

50g pistachios

50g cornflour

50g plain flour

1 tsp baking powder

50g unsalted butter

For the marzipan

125g ground almonds

125g icing sugar, plus more to dust

1 egg white or 2 tbsp Two Chicks liquid egg white

½ tsp almond extract

a few drops of pink gel food colour

Continued on page 63…

1. To make the custard for the crème pâtissière, heat the milk with the vanilla extract in a saucepan. While the milk is heating, whisk the egg yolks, cornflour and sugar by hand in a bowl. Once the milk is hot (but not boiling) pour it over the egg yolk mixture, whisking continually. Once combined, pour this back into the saucepan and return to the hob over a low heat. Continue mixing until the custard has thickened, then remove from the heat. Melt the butter in a pan or in a microwave for about 45 seconds on full power. (Remember to cover the butter with something so it doesn't spit all over your microwave.) Fold this into the custard. Pour the custard into a bowl, place cling film directly on to the surface to stop a skin forming and put in the fridge to chill.

2. Make the pistachio syrup by blitzing the pistachios in a food processor to a fine consistency. Mix them into the sugar and 100ml of water in a small saucepan. Heat until the syrup has reduced to a thicker consistency, then pour through a sieve into a bowl and leave to cool.

3. Preheat the oven to 180°C/fan 160°C/gas 4. Line the base of a 23cm springform cake tin with baking parchment. Make the sponge by whisking the eggs and sugar in a bowl with an electric whisk until a light-coloured foam has formed (this should take about 5 minutes).

4. Finely blitz the pistachios in the food processor and mix this with the flours and the baking powder in a separate bowl. Gently fold the egg and sugar mix into this. Melt the butter in a pan or in the microwave as above and fold this into the mixture. It will be much wetter than a regular sponge mix. Tip the batter into the prepared tin and bake for 25–30 minutes; it will be cooked when a cocktail stick stuck into the centre comes out dry. Put on a wire rack to cool. After 10 minutes, release the springform sides (you may need to free the edges with a knife first). Clean and dry the tin.

5. Make the marzipan: put the ground almonds and icing sugar in a food processor and mix thoroughly. Add the egg white, almond extract and food colour and mix well until all the ingredients come together. If you don't want to use unpasteurised egg white, use Two Chicks instead; it's available in most supermarkets. When the marzipan has formed, wrap in cling film to prevent it drying out.

6. To assemble, cut the cooled sponge in half using a cake-cutting wire or a long, sharp, serrated knife. Save the neatest half for the top.

To assemble

150g strawberries, hulled and
halved symmetrically down
the middle

For the jelly

100g strawberries, hulled
and chopped
25g caster sugar
1 sheet of gelatine

To decorate

50g white chocolate

Tool Kit

food processor
23cm springform cake tin
electric whisk
wire cooling rack
cake-cutting wire (optional)
pastry brush
piping bags
rolling pin
offset palette knife
serving plate or cake board

Line the clean springform tin with cling film and place one of the halves of sponge in the bottom. Brush some pistachio syrup on to the sponge. Take the halved strawberries and place them – cut side out – around the edge of the tin, with the tip facing up.

7. Return to the crème pâtissière: whip the cream until it forms soft peaks and fold into the now-cooled custard. Load this into a piping bag and pipe on to the sponge, being careful not to get any on the cut sides of the strawberries or the finished effect won't look as sharp. The custard needs to come up as high as the tops of the strawberries. Smooth the custard out with an offset palette knife and place the second half of sponge on this. Brush on more pistachio syrup.

8. Roll out the marzipan to around 5mm thick, using icing sugar rather than flour to dust the worktop. Lay the marzipan on top of the sponge and trim the edges. You can now gently press the cake down so the surface of the marzipan is about 5mm below the top edge of the springform tin. (This ensures the custard fills the cake, and makes room for the jelly layer.)

9. Make the jelly by cooking the strawberries gently with the caster sugar in a small pan. While this is heating, soak the gelatine in water to soften, then add to the strawberries and sugar. Mix thoroughly, then pour through a sieve on to the marzipan layer. Put the cake in the fridge for at least 1 hour for the jelly to set and the cake to firm up. Take the cake out of the fridge, release the springform sides and very gently take off the cling film (this is a bit fiddly, but it does come off eventually; take your time).

10. Melt the white chocolate for decoration in a heatproof bowl over a small saucepan of water over a medium-low heat (make sure the water doesn't touch the bowl). When the chocolate has melted, load it into a piping bag and cut a very small hole. Decorate the top of the cake with the white chocolate. Place on a serving plate or cake board.

11. Er, what are you waiting for? You've earned this!

Extras

So, fraisier cake. Not that bad, is it? This is the version I like, but there are plenty of variations, if you fancy.

Try different flavours of syrup to brush on the sponge: making syrups is pretty easy as long as you go for two parts water to one part sugar, plus your flavour.

Put any kind of fruit you want in, as long as it's soft.

The sponge can be any flavour you like, as long your sugar weighs the same as the flours mixed with any blitzed nuts (in this case 150g). Rather than pistachio, it also tastes very good with ground almonds. You can make the sponge nut-free, too, by just using half cornflour and half plain flour.

HAZELNUT CHOCOLATE OPERA CAKE

STAR BAKE

This is proper showstopper territory: lots of techniques, lots of layers and lots of flavour. It's great fun to make if you enjoy building things, as I do, and requires a steady hand and good attention to detail. Of all the things I make, this is the cake where people usually say 'It's a good job you're a builder', as it's a bit like constructing a wall out of cake... using an offset palette knife instead of a trowel. Before you start this cake, make sure you can fit your cake tin on a shelf in the freezer.

MAKES 1 | SERVES 10–12
Ingredients
For the praline
100g caster sugar
100g whole blanched hazelnuts

For the chocolate ganache
300ml double cream
300g dark chocolate (70 per cent cocoa solids)

For the sponge
6 large eggs
100g caster sugar, plus more to sprinkle
a little vegetable oil, for the tin
100g plain flour

For the Italian meringue buttercream
180g caster sugar
3 large egg whites
300g unsalted butter, at room temperature
60ml hazelnut liqueur (such as Fratello)

For the coffee syrup
4 tsp instant coffee
60ml coffee liqueur (such as Kahlúa)

1. Start by making the hazelnut praline. Pour the caster sugar into a heavy-based saucepan and heat gently. You may need to swirl the sugar around a bit to help it melt evenly, but try not to stir it. Once it has melted and taken on a very light yellow colour, tip the hazelnuts into the pan, take off the heat, and swirl around to cover all the nuts. If it thickens up too much to coat them, just heat up again to melt the sugar. Pour the coated hazelnuts on to a baking tray lined with baking parchment, scraping as much sugar out of the pan as possible, and set aside to cool completely. It will look at though you have ruined your pan forever. You haven't. Just pour water in, heat it over the hob and the hardened caramel will dissolve.

2. Next make the ganache, by first pouring the cream into a saucepan, then setting it on the hob to boil (yes, boil). Break the chocolate into a heatproof bowl and pour the boiling cream over. Stir with a silicone spatula until combined, dark and glossy. Pour three-quarters of this into a large piping bag and set aside to cool. Leave the remaining one-quarter in the bowl.

3. Now for the sponge. Preheat the oven to 200°C/fan 180°C/gas 6. Put 3 eggs and 50g of the caster sugar in the bowl of a stand mixer fitted with the whisk attachment and whisk until light-coloured and airy; this should take 5–7 minutes.

4. Meanwhile, line the base of a lightly oiled large (about 40 x 27cm) Swiss roll tin with baking parchment. Put the now-cooled praline into a food processor and blitz it to dust. Take 50g of this and mix in a bowl with 50g of the plain flour until all of the stuck-together lumps of praline have broken down. Reserve the remaining praline in an airtight container for the top of the cake. Using a silicone spatula, gently fold the flour mixture into the whisked egg mixture, making sure there is no dry stuff left in the bottom. Pour into the prepared tin and spread out with the spatula. Bake for 8 minutes, or until golden brown on top. (It will brown quickly, due to the praline.)

5. Take out of the oven and leave to cool for 5 minutes, then sprinkle a fine layer of caster sugar on to a sheet of baking parchment. Tip the sponge on to this and peel off the baking parchment that it was cooked on (this will be a bit tricky, but be gentle and persevere). Repeat steps 3–5 to make a second sponge.

Tool Kit

baking tray
large piping bags
stand mixer fitted with
    whisk attachment
large Swiss roll tin (about
    40 x 27cm)
food processor
confectionery thermometer
pastry brush
18cm square cake tin or
    adjustable cake tin (this is
    a really useful tool)
offset palette knife
serving plate or cake board

6. For the buttercream, put 150g of the caster sugar and 60ml of water into a small saucepan with a cooking thermometer and set over a medium heat. Every now and again, brush down the sugar on the edges of the saucepan with a wet pastry brush. Do not stir! Meanwhile, beat the 3 egg whites with the remaining 30g of caster sugar in the (cleaned) bowl of your stand mixer, on medium speed.

7. Once the sugar on the hob reaches 110°C, set the stand mixer to high speed and beat the egg mixture until it reaches stiff peaks. Once the sugar reaches 118°C ('soft ball' stage), set the stand mixer to full power and slowly pour the sugar into the bowl, making sure not to pour it on to the moving whisk or you'll just get hard sugar crusting on the sides. Keep the mixer running on full until the bowl has cooled down completely; this should take about 10 minutes so can be a bit noisy! While the mixture is cooling, chop the butter and add, chunk by chunk, to the cooled meringue (still on high speed). Once all the butter is combined, pour in the hazelnut liqueur, scrape down the sides of the bowl and load into a piping bag. Set aside, but do not put in the fridge or it will firm up too much to work with.

8. Make the coffee syrup by mixing the instant coffee in a cup with 60ml of boiling water and the coffee liqueur.

9. To assemble, line an 18cm square cake tin (or adjustable cake tin set at 18cm) with cling film and cut the sponges into 4 x 18cm squares. Carefully lay the first into the tin (making sure not to pull down the cling film) and use a pastry brush to soak it in one-quarter of the coffee syrup. Pipe one-third of the buttercream on top and smooth out with an offset palette knife. Freeze for 10 minutes to firm up.

10. Remove from the freezer, pipe one-quarter of the ganache on top and smooth out with the offset palette knife.

11. Repeat, building up the layers until everything is used up. (Though you will still have the one-quarter of the ganache that you set aside in the bowl earlier.) From the bottom it will be:
    syrup-brushed sponge > buttercream > ganache > syrup-brushed sponge > buttercream > ganache > syrup-brushed sponge > buttercream > ganache > syrup-brushed sponge.
    Return this to the freezer for about 1 hour to set.

12. Take the cake out of the freezer and pour the remaining chocolate ganache from the bowl on top. Allow to set at room temperature.

13. Remove the cake from the tin, peel off the cling film and (if you feel like it) cut about 5mm off the edges to expose the sharp layers. You might as well show people the effort you have made...

14. Transfer to a serving plate or cake board. Traditionally, these cakes have 'opera' piped on the top, but I like to sprinkle over the remaining praline in an even layer (see overleaf). Show off to anyone who stands still long enough.

Continued...

Extras

Fourteen steps, eh? Now, that is a long one! This cake is an absolute winner. All the components can be scaled up or down depending on what size cake you want to make with no difference in cooking time, so feel free to make a monster if you feel like it. I've made this with hazelnut liqueur, mainly because I try to find an excuse to put it in most things I make at the moment.

There are a few pitfalls that you may encounter, so here's how to repair the most common:

The Italian meringue buttercream can sometimes split when you're adding the butter (it will look like cottage cheese). To repair this, just take 3–4 tbsp out of the mixture and microwave for 10–20 seconds, then return the melted liquid to the mixture, beating on high speed; this will get the buttercream back pretty much every time.

You might find your ganache splits when you're mixing in the cream. To remedy this, just whisk on a high speed until it re-combines.

Other than those two fixes, this recipe should be plain sailing.

4

CELEBRATION CAKES

LEMON AND POPPY SEED BIRTHDAY CAKE

LEVEL 1

So, it's your mate's birthday and they're coming round in a couple of hours. They casually mention that no one got them a birthday cake this year. Sounds like a massive hint to me, considering they know you've just bought this awesome book. This is an emergency birthday cake that is straightforward to make and tastes brilliant. Lemon and poppy seed has long been a favourite of mine, whether it's in birthday cake form, or as a massive tray bake that the kids can go mad decorating. The ingredients are simple and it requires no ridiculous equipment to make. So when you're in a bind, or if you just fancy a really nice cake, make this. It's yum.

SERVES 8
Ingredients
For the sponge
225g unsalted butter, softened, plus more for the tins
225g caster sugar
4 large eggs
225g plain flour
2 tsp baking powder
finely grated zest of 3 unwaxed lemons, reserving a few slivers for decoration, plus the juice of 1
50g poppy seeds

For the icing
50g unsalted butter, softened
100g cream cheese
400g icing sugar
2 tbsp lemon juice

Tool Kit
2 x 20cm round sandwich tins
electric whisk
wire cooling rack
cake-cutting wire (optional)
offset palette knife

1. Preheat the oven to 180°C/fan 160°C/gas 4. Butter 2 x 20cm round sandwich tins and line the bases with baking parchment.

2. In a large bowl, beat together the sugar and butter with an electric whisk until light-coloured and creamy. Beat in the eggs one by one, beating thoroughly between each addition. If the mixture starts to split, just add 1 tbsp of the flour and continue beating; this will bring the mixture back.

3. Sift together the flour and baking powder and fold into the mixture with the finely grated lemon zest and poppy seeds, making sure to mix in any flour at the bottom of the bowl. Be gentle when you're folding; you don't want to knock out the air you've incorporated through all that whisking. Fold in the lemon juice and divide the batter evenly between the prepared tins, smoothing the surfaces. Bake for 18–20 minutes, or until a cocktail stick comes out clean when poked into the centre of each cake. When the tins have cooled enough to handle, turn out the sponges and cool on a wire rack.

4. Meanwhile, prepare the icing. Beat together the butter and cream cheese in a large bowl with the electric whisk until creamy and fully combined. Beat in half the icing sugar (start your whisk on slow, or you'll get icing sugar all over the kitchen). Beat in the lemon juice, then gradually beat in the rest of the icing sugar, a couple of spoonfuls at a time, until it's a thick-but-spreadable consistency.

5. Once the sponges have cooled, use a cake-cutting wire or a serrated knife to slice off the raised middles of the cakes (I usually spread a bit of the icing on these as a secret personal preview). Spread about half the icing on the bottom layer of sponge using an offset palette knife. Try to spread it evenly and right up to the edges, so you can see a neat line of icing once the top goes on. Turn the top layer of sponge upside down and lay on top of the icing, pressing down gently and scraping off any excess icing that squidges out.

6. Using the offset palette knife, neatly spread the remaining icing on top and decorate with the remaining slivers of zest. Invite your friend in and pretend it was no big deal. Which, of course, is true.

Continued...

Extras

This recipe works really well as an everyday cake, as you can knock it out quickly, but you can scale it up quite easily, too. If you don't have 20cm sandwich tins, you can just as easily make it in 23cm cake tins, using 6 eggs, 350g each of caster sugar, butter and flour, 3 tsp of baking powder, 4 lemons and 75g poppy seeds. Bake for 25-30 minutes and test as usual.

I really like making this recipe as a tray bake with the kids, as I can leave them to drizzle it with lemon icing, then sprinkle half my decorating bits and pieces over the top. (Kids often favour quantity over beauty when it comes to decoration, so only put out as many decorations as you're willing to lose!)

Plain lemon glacé icing is much easier to make than this cream cheese version, just mix 1-2 tbsp of lemon juice with 150g of icing sugar and drizzle it on the cake.

If you're looking to add another element to this cake, why not stir 100g of blueberries through the mixture, instead of the poppy seeds? Make sure you wash the berries and roll them in a dusting of flour before adding to the batter, though, or they'll all sink to the bottom.

MADEIRA CAKE WITH FONDANT DECORATING TECHNIQUES

Madeira cake is perfect as the base for a birthday cake. Its dense structure holds more strongly than Victoria sponge, so it's good for large, tiered cakes, too. If you master this simple recipe, you'll never need to buy a shop-bought kids' birthday cake again. It was through experimenting with my daughters' birthday cakes that I got into baking more often, as you don't need much artistic flair to make a great-looking cake (there are so many templates online). When it comes to fondant, I prefer to use shop-bought. As with filo pastry, it's one of those things where home-made is a lot of effort and never quite as good. I strongly recommend gel food colours for fondant: you get a much stronger, more vivid colour without making the fondant wet and sticky. I recommend the Wilton pack of eight colours, available online; they last for ages.

SERVES 8 GROWN UPS OR 12 CHILDREN

Ingredients

For the cake

350g unsalted butter, at room temperature, plus more for the tins

350g caster sugar

6 large eggs

2 tsp vanilla bean paste

400g plain flour

1 tsp baking powder

finely grated zest of 2 unwaxed lemons

For filling and icing the cake

about 100g strawberry jam

150g unsalted butter, at room temperature

400g icing sugar, plus more to dust

1–2 tbsp milk, if needed

gel food colours

1kg ready-to-roll white fondant icing

Continued overleaf...

1. Preheat the oven to 180°C/fan 160°C/gas 4. Butter 2 x 20cm round sandwich tins and line the bases with baking parchment.

2. In a large bowl, cream together the sugar and butter with an electric whisk until light-coloured and fluffy. Thoroughly beat in each egg, one by one, along with the vanilla bean paste. If it starts to split, add 1 tbsp of the flour and beat again to bring it back together. Sift the flour and baking powder together and fold into the wet mixture with a silicone spatula, along with the lemon zest.

3. Divide the batter equally between the prepared tins, smooth it out with an offset palette knife and bake for 45–50 minutes, or until a cocktail stick comes out clean when stuck into the centre of each cake. Keep an eye on the top of the cakes towards the end of the bake and, if they are browning too quickly, cover them with foil. Take out of the oven and place on a wire rack until cool enough to turn out of the tins, then allow to cool completely.

4. To construct, cut the tops off the Madeira sponges to make them both flat. Lay the bottom sponge on a 25cm round cake board. Spread on the strawberry jam and lay the top sponge on top of this, bottom side up. There will be a bit of a gap between the two sponges but you'll fill this with buttercream.

5. To make the buttercream, beat the butter in a large bowl with the electric whisk until soft. Gradually add 300g of the icing sugar and continue to mix, adding the milk if you need to loosen the mixture. You can add food colour to this if you want. Coat the cake, sides and top with buttercream, using the offset palette knife to make it smooth all around.

6. Take three-quarters of the fondant to cover the cake and leave the remainder, wrapped well in cling film so it doesn't dry out, for additional decorations. For my 'pirate face' cake (see page 75), I mix a little ivory (or pink) gel food colour into the fondant.

Tool Kit

2 x 20cm round sandwich tins
electric whisk
offset palette knife
wire cooling rack
25cm round cake board
rolling pin
cake/icing smoother
   (optional)
piping bag (optional)

Roll the fondant out to a circle 3–5mm thick and large enough to cover the top and sides of the cake. Carefully roll this on to the rolling pin, then unroll it over the top of the cake. Smooth the fondant icing across the top and sides (I use a cake/icing smoother to help with this). Trim the excess icing from the bottom of the cake. The fondant icing should stick to the buttercream and stay in place.

7. Colour the remaining fondant icing for the rest of the decorations. For my pirate face, I make a pirate bandana and its polka dots, eye patch, eye, nose, mouth, hair and freckles. Stick these pieces on to the cake with a little water.

8. Finally, if you want to add a birthday greeting, knock up a little glacé icing with the remaining 100g of icing sugar, food colour and a tiny bit of water: add just ½ tsp at a time and keep mixing until smooth. Load into a piping bag and pipe a greeting on to the cake board. Serve the cake to the grateful birthday girl or boy, who will think you're a hero!

Extras

Once you've got the hang of the Madeira sponge and the initial layer of fondant icing, this cake is a doddle. It doesn't need refrigerating, so keeps well if you make it the day before a party, while the buttercream icing holds it together well in a party bag. It's a blank canvas for whatever you want to do. I would recommend using the website Pinterest for templates and ideas for favourite TV characters or other designs.

SIMNEL CAKE

My mother-in-law makes Simnel cake at Easter, or on Mother's Day as a mid-fasting treat. She usually gives up chocolate for Lent, so this is a great cake to get into her good books as it's really sweet but without any chocolate. Simnel cakes have a long cooking time, but are well worth the wait.

SERVES 11

Ingredients

For the marzipan

250g ground almonds

250g icing sugar

2 large egg whites, or 4 tbsp
    Two Chicks liquid
    egg white

1 tsp almond extract

For the cake

175g unsalted butter, at room
    temperature, plus more for
    the tin

175g light soft brown sugar

3 large eggs

225g plain flour

1 tsp baking powder

2 tsp ground allspice

150g raisins

150g sultanas

75g candied mixed peel

finely grated zest of 1 unwaxed
    lemon and 1 orange

50g apricot jam

Tool Kit

food processor (for the
    marzipan)

20cm loose-bottomed
    deep-sided round
    sandwich tin

electric whisk

offset palette knife (optional)

wire cooling rack

pastry brush

1. Start by making the marzipan in a food processor, as on page 61, but without the food colour. Wrap in cling film to prevent it drying out and put it in the fridge. Preheat the oven to 150°C/fan 130°C/gas 2.

2. Butter a 20cm loose-bottomed round sandwich tin. Line with baking parchment.

3. Beat together the sugar and butter with an electric whisk until smooth, light-coloured and creamy. Beat in the eggs one by one, beating thoroughly between each addition. If the mixture starts to split, put 1 tbsp of the flour in to bring it back and continue to beat.

4. Sift together the flour, baking powder and allspice and gently fold them in. Then fold in the raisins, sultanas, mixed peel and zests; be gentle, as you don't want to knock too much air out of the mixture.

5. Tip half the batter into the tin and smooth with a spatula or offset palette knife. Roll out 150g of the chilled marzipan into a circle just smaller than the tin and lay it on. Spread the remaining batter on top. It will come quite far up, but don't worry – it will cook just fine.

6. Cook in the oven for 2½ hours (yes, that long, as the marzipan slows the cooking of the batter beneath it). Check in the last 30 minutes and if it has browned too much, pop some foil over the top. Leave to cool on a wire rack for 30 minutes. Turn out and leave until cold.

7. Heat up the jam in a saucepan with 1 tbsp of water until boiling. Paint the jam on the top of the cake with a pastry brush. Roll out 250g of the marzipan into a 20cm circle and lay on the cake (using the jam as glue). Score a criss-cross pattern on it and crimp the edges.

8. Roll the remaining marzipan into 11 even-sized balls and place them evenly around the edge, sticking down with a dab more jam. Put the cake under a medium grill and lightly brown the top of the marzipan: make sure you take it out before it gets too brown.

Extras

You could whack in 150g glacé cherries (quarter them, wash, dry and roll them in flour to stop them sinking). Or it could easily take 75g of flaked almonds. I like to eat this with a handful of sugared almonds, but I'm sharing a little too much of my potentially life-threatening almond addiction (one day at a time...).

To make a bigger cake, add an extra egg, add one-third on to all the other ingredients and bake it in a 23cm tin for the same time, as the depth is the same.

Now you can make marzipan, you're freed from the rock-hard ball in the cupboard that results from buying it. To make smaller quantities, I recommend you buy liquid egg white. It's also brilliant for macarons (see page 100).

'FREE FROM' ORANGE AND ALMOND CAKE

I get loads of requests for 'free from' recipes. I used to be quite wary of them, thinking that cutting out tried-and-tested ingredients would result in lack of flavour or disappointing textures. I was glad to be proved wrong by recipes from friends and family. The beauty of this variation I came up with is that it's not just gluten-free, but also dairy-free.

SERVES 8–10

Ingredients

For the orange curd

3 large eggs

90ml runny honey

finely grated zest and juice of
    1 large orange

75g coconut oil, plus more for
    the tin

For the cake

2 large oranges

5 eggs, separated

200g caster sugar

1 tsp almond extract

225g ground almonds

50g flaked almonds

icing sugar, to serve

Tool Kit

food processor (optional)

23cm springform cake tin

wire cooling rack

cake-cutting wire (optional)

1. First make the curd. Beat together the eggs and honey in a heavy-based saucepan. Add the orange zest and juice and the coconut oil and place over a gentle heat, all the time keeping the mixture moving. Do not be tempted to turn up the heat to speed up the process, or you will end up with orange-flavoured scrambled eggs. Keep heating and mixing until the mixture thickens. This should not take long (about 10 minutes). Once thickened, pass the curd through a sieve into a bowl, cover with cling film and leave in the fridge.

2. Next make the cake: chop the oranges (unpeeled, but remove any pips) and heat in a saucepan with a couple of tbsp of water. Cover and cook over a low heat for 30 minutes. Keep an eye on the oranges, or they will stick and burn. Once cooked, blitz to a pulp in a food processor, or finely chop, then put in the fridge for 30 minutes.

3. Preheat the oven to 200°C/fan 180°C/gas 6. Line a 23cm springform tin with baking parchment, using coconut oil to stick it to the tin.

4. Whisk the egg whites with half the sugar until stiff peaks form. In another bowl, whisk the egg yolks with the remaining sugar and the almond extract until they become light and glossy.

5. Gently fold the cooled puréed oranges and ground almonds into the yolk mixture. Fold in the egg whites, a few spoonfuls at a time, to retain as much lightness as possible.

6. Pour into the prepared tin, smooth out, sprinkle the flaked almonds on top and bake for 50–60 minutes. Keep an eye on it for the last 20 minutes; you may need to cover it with foil if it starts burning.

7. Check the cake is cooked through: a cocktail stick poked in the centre should come out clean. Release from the tin and set on a cooling rack.

8. Once cool, cut the cake in half with a cake-cutting wire or serrated knife, spread the cooled orange curd on the bottom half and put the other half on top. Sprinkle with icing sugar and serve.

Extras

This is a great after-dinner cake and goes really well with a glass of amaretto.

If you don't need it to be dairy-free, it also works with a bit of mascarpone cream or vanilla ice cream on the side.

You can also turn it into a chocolate-orange cake by whisking 50g cocoa powder into the egg yolk mixture and reducing the ground almonds to 200g.

CHRISTMAS CAKE

This is a cake you are pretty much guaranteed to make every year. Last year I made three and still managed to eat only one measly slice! The recipe does benefit from being made a few weeks in advance (I usually start mine just after Bonfire Night) so you can soak it in booze, but also works just fine if you've left it to the last minute. I've given a version that uses royal icing, but if you don't have the time or the inclination – or if you just like it better – use fondant instead (see page 73). As a kid, we always used to make a big deal of baking the Christmas cake and everyone in the family had to give it a stir for good luck. I still do that now with my own family.

SERVES 10–12
Ingredients
For the cake

75g glacé cherries

250g currants

250g raisins

250g sultanas

75g candied mixed peel

finely grated zest of 1 orange
and 1 unwaxed lemon

60ml brandy, plus more to
'feed' the cake

225g unsalted butter, at
room temperature

1 tsp vanilla bean paste

225g dark soft brown sugar

4 eggs

225g plain flour

½ tsp freshly grated nutmeg

1 tsp mixed spice

75g blanched almonds,
finely chopped

For the marzipan layer

100g apricot jam

1 quantity Marzipan (page 76)

a little cornflour, to dust

For the royal icing

3 large egg whites or 6 tbsp
Two Chicks liquid egg white

1 tbsp lemon juice

500g icing sugar

Continued on page 80...

1. Start the day before you want to make the cake by soaking the fruit. Cut the glacé cherries up into eighths and put in a bowl with the currants, raisins, sultanas, mixed peel and zests. Pour in the brandy and stir together with a wooden spoon until all the fruit is wet. Some brandy will collect in the bottom of the bowl. Cover with cling film and leave to soak overnight.

2. When you're ready to make the cake and know you've got a few hours spare to bake it, prepare an 18cm square or adjustable cake tin, or a 20cm round, deep-sided cake tin, by lining it with double layers of baking parchment. You'll need to fold the baking parchment up the sides of the tin and fold it over the top rim to make it hold in place. Preheat the oven to 160°C/fan 140°C/gas 3.

3. Cream together the butter, vanilla bean paste and sugar in a large bowl with an electric whisk until smooth and light in colour. Beat in the eggs one by one, beating thoroughly between each addition. If the mixture starts to split, just beat in 1 tbsp of the flour to bring it back.

4. Sift together the flour, nutmeg and mixed spice and gently fold into the batter with a silicone spatula, making sure to pick up any flour that collects in the bottom of the bowl. Tip in the soaked fruit and almonds and gently fold together until the cake is well mixed (get everyone else to do it too for good luck!). Gently tip into the prepared tin (don't let it hit the parchment-lined sides and drag them down as it is poured in) and smooth out flat with an offset palette knife.

5. Lay a double layer of baking parchment with a small hole cut into the middle directly on top of the batter, then bake for 4–4½ hours. After 4 hours, poke a cocktail stick into the centre of the cake to check if it is cooked. If it's cooked the stick will come out clean. Put the cake on a wire rack in its tin for 1 hour to cool down.

6. Once cool enough to handle, remove the cake from the tin and set on the cooling rack to cool fully. Poke several holes in the top of the cake with a skewer (to help it absorb booze), wrap in foil and put in an airtight container. Every few days in the weeks before Christmas, sprinkle a little brandy directly on to the cake to soak in, then wrap it up again.

Christmas Cake continued...

Tool Kit

18cm square or adjustable
   cake tin, or 20cm
   diameter round
   sandwich tin
electric whisk
offset palette knife
wire cooling rack
cake board or serving plate
rolling pin
pastry brush
cake/icing smoother
   (optional)

7. Put the jam in a saucepan with 2 tbsp of water and set on a low heat to melt together. Once the jam is melted, take off the heat and set aside. Unwrap the cake and set it on a cake board or serving plate.

8. Take the marzipan out of the fridge and roll out on a cornflour-dusted work surface to a 35cm square (it's less likely to stick to cornflour than it is to icing sugar). While rolling, turn it regularly and, if necessary, sprinkle more cornflour to stop it sticking. Use a pastry brush to paint a thick layer of jam all over the cake (clean the drips that land on your cake board with damp kitchen paper).

9. Roll the marzipan up on to the rolling pin and lay on to the cake. Working as quickly as you can, push the marzipan on to the edges of the cake. Be careful to avoid tearing it on the corners (if it does, patch it with some offcuts). Cut excess marzipan off the bottom and smooth the surface with a cake/icing smoother, if you like.

10. Now make the royal icing by putting the egg whites and lemon juice in a large bowl and beating in the icing sugar with the electric whisk on a low speed, a couple of spoonfuls at a time. Then turn the whisk up to high speed and beat until the mixture thickens.

11. Using an offset palette knife, liberally spread the icing all over. Draw it into peaks with the back of a spoon. Leave to set. Serve on Christmas Day.

Extras

I love Christmas and making Christmas food. I understand, however, that not everyone does, so here are a few shortcuts you can rely on if you've really got to go out and get shopping, or go mad at a work Christmas party.

Firstly, although I really urge you to make it, you can always buy marzipan. It comes ready to roll. It is also usually found in the back of the cupboard, opened and rock-hard from last year, so if you do have any left over, make marzipan fruits with it with the kids, or build it into the sweet baking recipes in this book.

If you don't fancy royal icing, you can buy fondant icing in a packet. It's an easy way to cover cakes quickly and neatly. Remember to put another layer of melted jam on the marzipan to stick it on, though. You may get the odd tear in it if you roll it out too thinly, but in most cases, you can rub a bit of icing into the tear with your cake-smoothing tool and no one will know. If you have an imperfection you can't smooth over, it's time to do some creative decorating. One thing you should avoid with fondant icing is water; it will melt the icing.

If you don't fancy marzipan or icing, I've got you covered. After you've baked the cake and fed it for a couple of weeks, toast a few nuts (blanched almonds, walnuts and pecans work well) paint a layer of jam on the cake and arrange the nuts on it. Paint more jam on the nuts to glaze them and you're done.

PEACH AND WHITE CHOCOLATE OMBRÉ CAKE

This is my wife's favourite cake, and as such deserves its place in this book without any further introduction. But I suppose you might need a little bit more information on it, so here it is. The combination of the sweet peach and super-creamy frosting makes for what I consider to be a more grown-up-tasting cake: not over-sweet, but far too moreish. Have fun making this and give it to someone special.

SERVES 10
Ingredients
For the peach purée
8 ripe peaches (they *must* be ripe)
2 tbsp lemon juice
½ tsp vanilla bean paste
1 tsp almond extract

For the white chocolate frosting
300g white chocolate
300ml double cream
250g cream cheese
edible gold spray

For the sponge
350g unsalted butter, at room temperature, plus more for the tins
350g caster sugar
3 tsp vanilla bean paste
6 large eggs
350g plain flour
3 tsp baking powder
3 x 10g tubes of orange gel food colour (use tubes rather than pots in this case, as you need to make sure each layer has the right amount of colour)

Continued on page 84…

1. To start, make the peach purée by dropping the peaches in furiously boiling water (obviously don't drop them from a height!) and boiling them for 2–3 minutes. Take the peaches out of the water with a slotted spoon and put into a large bowl of cold water to cool down for 5 minutes. Take the peaches out of the water and peel them; the skin should be loose and should peel off easily. If it doesn't, your peaches are probably not ripe enough. You can still make the cake, but you'll need to use a potato peeler on the peaches and keep an extra eye on them when cooking.

2. Once the peaches are peeled, quarter and stone them and put them in a saucepan (this will be a sticky business but, trust me, it's worth it!). Add the lemon juice, vanilla bean paste and almond extract and set over a low heat, stirring occasionally. Cook for 10–15 minutes, then leave to cool.

3. Make the frosting by breaking the white chocolate into a heatproof bowl. Pour the double cream into a saucepan and bring to the boil over a medium heat. Once boiling, immediately pour the cream over the chocolate and mix with a silicone spatula until combined. Leave in the fridge until completely chilled (about 1 hour).

4. Butter 2 x 20cm round sandwich tins and line with baking parchment. (You'll be using these tins again, so cut 6 identical pieces of parchment.) Preheat the oven to 180°C/fan 160°C/gas 4.

5. In a large bowl, beat together the butter and sugar using an electric whisk until light and fluffy. Add the vanilla bean paste and beat in the eggs, one by one. If the mixture starts to split, just add 1 tbsp of the flour. Sift together the baking powder and flour and fold into the wet mixture, making sure to pick up all the flour from the sides and base of the bowl. You have now made enough batter for 6 thin sponges.

6. Put a clean bowl on the kitchen scales and weigh out 225g of batter. Transfer this to the first sandwich tin and smooth the surface out with an offset palette knife.

Tool Kit

2 x 20cm round sandwich tins
electric whisk
offset palette knife
wire cooling rack
cake-cutting wire (optional)
cake board or serving plate

7. Weigh out another 225g of batter into the bowl and add the food colour (this will be the lightest orange layer); about 30 drops will do. Gently mix the colour in. Transfer to the second sandwich tin and smooth out with the offset palette knife. Bake both cakes for 15–20 minutes, or until a cocktail stick comes out clean when poked into the centre of each cake. Turn out on to a wire rack to cool.

8. Wash, dry, butter and re-line the sandwich tins. Weigh out the next batch of cake batter, this time tinting one with 60 drops of colour and the other with 90. Bake and turn out in the same way as before. Bake the final 2 sponges, coloured with 120 drops and 150 drops respectively.

9. Finish off the peach purée by blitzing in a blender until smooth. Set aside. Take the cooled white chocolate ganache out of the fridge and beat for 5 minutes using the electric whisk: soft peaks will form and the volume will increase as air is incorporated. Whisk in the cream cheese and set aside.

10. Use a cake-cutting wire, or a serrated knife, to cut the top off each sponge where it had risen during baking. This also makes it easier to see which shade of orange they are if you have muddled them up!

11. Take the deepest-orange sponge and place on your cake board or plate. Using a small spatula, spread a thin layer of frosting evenly on top. Next spread about one-fifth of the peach purée on to the frosting. Carefully spread another thin layer of frosting on to the *bottom* of the next sponge and lay it on top of the first. (The purée is held between layers of frosting to stop it from soaking into the sponge and making it sticky.)

12. Continue to layer the sponge, frosting and purée layers until you have laid the final, undyed sponge on the top, then start to cover the whole cake evenly with the rest of the frosting.

13. Run the end of a palette knife around the cake to form a spiral indent pattern over the surface. Lightly spray with edible gold food colouring to pick out the pattern. Put in the fridge and serve, chilled, when you like.

Extras

These cake layers offer a brilliant effect that looks ace when cut into, but need loads and loads of colour. I like to put as many layers in as I can, as height here is a real winner (I work it out at one egg per layer). Try making the ganache frosting with milk or dark chocolate if you fancy. I really like using very simple fruit purées for this cake: raspberry or blackcurrant offer a really zingy sharpness that works brilliantly with the smooth ganache.

BLACK FOREST GATEAU

My guilty secret. I don't even eat it like an ironic hipster; I just eat it because it tastes and looks great. So clear your head of any 1970s nightmares you might have conjured up: there's no squirty UHT cream or glacé cherries here, just chocolatey, morello cherry-ey goodness. Let's get cracking...

SERVES 10–12

Ingredients

For the filling and decoration

400g black cherries in syrup (drained weight; these come in a can of around 850g)

320g (1 regular jar) morello cherry jam

2 tbsp kirsch

2 tbsp arrowroot

600ml double cream

250g dark chocolate (70 per cent cocoa solids)

12 ripe cherries with stalks

For the sponge

350g unsalted butter, softened, plus more for the tin

350g caster sugar

6 large eggs

100g dark chocolate (70 per cent cocoa solids)

300g plain flour

4 tsp baking powder

50g cocoa powder

2 tbsp kirsch

6 tbsp cherry syrup (from the cherries in syrup)

Tool Kit

3 x 20cm round sandwich tins (or bake in batches)

electric whisk

offset palette knife

2 wire cooling racks

pastry brush

2 piping bags

display plate

1. Prepare the filling by first draining the canned black cherries, reserving the syrup in a bowl. Tip the cherries into a saucepan with the jam and kirsch. Bring to the boil; this should release quite a lot of juice. Take 3–4 tbsp of the juice and mix with the arrowroot to form a paste, then return the paste to the saucepan. Stir; it should thicken up quickly. As soon as it thickens, take off the heat and allow to cool.

2. To make the cakes, butter 3 x 20cm round sandwich tins and line the bases with baking parchment. (If you only have 1 or 2 tins, you can still make the cake, but you'll have to bake it in batches.) Beat together the sugar and butter with an electric whisk until light-coloured, smooth and creamy. Beat in the eggs one by one, beating well between each addition.

3. Put the 100g of dark chocolate for the cake in a heatproof bowl and set over a saucepan half-filled with simmering water (the bowl should not touch the water). Once melted, take off the heat to cool.

4. Sift together the flour, baking powder and cocoa powder into a separate bowl, then fold this into the egg mixture, making sure there is no unmixed flour left in the bottom of the bowl.

5. Preheat the oven to 180°C/fan 160°C/gas 4. Pour the chocolate into the mix and fold this in too, then load each of the prepared tins with 450g of the mix, spread out with an offset palette knife and bake for 18–20 minutes, or until a cocktail stick comes out clean when poked into the centre of each sponge. Put on 2 cooling racks and turn the sponges out of the tins once they are cool enough to handle. Leave the cakes on the racks until completely cold.

6. Once the cakes are cold, mix the kirsch with the 6 tbsp of cherry syrup and brush on the top of the cakes, dividing it evenly between them. Whisk 575ml of the cream until it forms firm peaks and set aside for decorating.

7. Melt 25g of the dark chocolate as before for decoration. Once melted, take off the heat. Mix in the remaining 25ml of double cream to form a small amount of ganache. Load into a piping bag.

8. Using a sharp knife, carefully cut around the indent of each ripe cherry and split open, being careful not to pull the stalk off. Pop the stone out of the cherry and pipe a blob of dark chocolate ganache in its place. Close the cherry up again (the setting ganache should seal it). Set aside.

Continued on page 87...

9. To make the chocolate decorations, roughly chop 100g of the remaining dark chocolate and melt as before. Meanwhile, finely chop the remaining 125g chocolate and set aside.

10. Stir the chocolate in the bowl to fully melt it down, and immediately take off the heat. Dry the base of the bowl and stir in half the finely chopped chocolate. This should take about 1 minute to melt into the mix. If it melts in more quickly than that, let the chocolate stand for 5 minutes to cool off. Now add the remaining finely chopped chocolate. This will temper the chocolate, so you can pipe it out into shapes that will set hard and shiny.

11. Lay out 2 sheets of baking parchment on a flat surface, dip each of the ganache-filled cherries into the chocolate and lay out to set.

12. Next, load the remaining melted chocolate into a piping bag. Pipe out trees of different heights on to the parchment. Try piping them out quite quickly, as you'll get a better effect than if you painstakingly try to make every tree perfect.

13. To assemble, place the bottom sponge on a display plate and spread on a thin layer of cream (about 5mm), then spread around half of the cooled cherry mix on top of that. Place the next sponge on top and layer cream and cherries on again. Place the final layer of sponge on top, upside down, so the layer that was soaked with syrup is facing down, and gently press to consolidate the cake.

14. Use the offset palette knife to cover the whole cake in the remaining cream and smooth out to an even surface. Because it is double cream you won't be able to make the surface totally smooth, but don't worry; it all adds to the effect!

15. Position the set chocolate trees around the sides and on top of the cake as densely as you like; pressing them into the cream. Arrange the chocolate cherries around the edge of the cake. Bingo!

Extras

If you have a confectionery thermometer, you can use it to help temper the chocolate here: while tempering, add the unmelted chocolate only when the melted chocolate has cooled to 46–48°C. This is the optimum temperature that allows a shiny hard chocolate to form. (For milk chocolate it is 40–45°C and for white chocolate it is 37–40°C.) Why not use all three types of chocolate for your forest?

I make chocolate ganache using the ratio of 1:1 cream to chocolate. Try making 600ml of ganache, chill it in the fridge, then whip. Whipped ganache covering tastes and looks brilliant; it goes further too, as the volume increases.

If you find the rawness of kirsch a bit jarring, use cherry brandy. (I'd happily pour that over most things!)

5

BISCUITS

COCONUT MACAROONS

When I was a kid, these were a real treat for me and my sisters. And they're nothing like a macaron (see page 100), as I wrongly assumed until I was about 25. These are lovely in their own right, if less fashionable, and *sooo* simple to make, so start your biscuit baking here and build your way up. They are also a good way to use up any extra egg whites left over from making custard.

MAKES 18–20
Ingredients
2 large egg whites
½ tsp vanilla bean paste
150g caster sugar
175g desiccated coconut
50g ground almonds
100g dark chocolate (70 per
    cent cocoa solids)

Tool Kit
electric whisk
2 baking trays or sheets
wire cooling rack
palette knife

1. Beat the egg whites, vanilla bean paste and sugar with an electric whisk until soft peaks form. Fold in the desiccated coconut and ground almonds, making sure they are fully incorporated and that there is no unmixed coconut at the bottom of the bowl. Leave to stand for 30 minutes.

2. Preheat the oven to 190°C/fan 170°C/gas 5. Line 2 baking trays or sheets with baking parchment.

3. Take about 1 tbsp of the mixture for each macaroon and shape them, on the prepared trays, into discs of about 5cm diameter, pressing down with the back of a fork to slightly flatten them and leave the impression of the tines in the tops.

4. Bake for 15–20 minutes, or until golden brown. Take out of the oven and allow to stand for 5 minutes before transferring to a wire rack with a palette knife to cool.

5. Set a heatproof bowl over a saucepan of water on a medium heat (the bowl must not touch the water). Break the chocolate into chunks and melt it in the bowl, stirring occasionally.

6. When the chocolate has melted, dip the top of each macaroon in it and return to the cooling rack to set.

Extras
This is the simple method for macaroons. If you find they are too sticky when you're shaping them, try wetting your hands. You don't have to dip them in chocolate, but my theory is that everything can take a little bit of chocolate, so why not? Try drizzling them with white or milk chocolate, too. You can replace the coconut completely with ground almonds if you like; pop a blanched almond on the top and cook in the same way.

LAVENDER SHORTBREAD

Last year my wife woke up one morning and told me we were taking the kids lavender picking at Hitchin Lavender Farm. 'Hooray,' I thought, a bit half-heartedly. The weather looked horrible and the children were grumpy, so the prospect didn't seem good. But it was brilliant! The kids spent the day legging it up and down rows of purple flowers while Sarah and I wandered around happily. Maybe it was the thick aroma of lavender, maybe it was the surprise enthusiasm of the littl'uns, maybe it was just a day of fresh air, but we all got home – with a massive bag of lavender – feeling like we'd won! These shortbread biscuits are one of the results of that day and they are lovely.

MAKES AROUND 20,
DEPENDING ON WHAT
COOKIE CUTTER YOU USE
Ingredients
200g unsalted butter, at
    room temperature
100g caster sugar
½ tsp table salt
1 tbsp lavender flowers
300g plain flour, plus more
    to dust

Tool Kit
electric whisk
rolling pin
cookie cutters (any shape)
baking tray or sheet
wire cooling rack
palette knife

1. Chop the butter, tip it into a bowl and beat to a creamy texture with an electric whisk. (If your butter is not at room temperature, chop it and put it into a jug with tepid water to soften up for 10 minutes, then drain the water out of the jug.) Add the sugar and salt and beat until soft and creamy.

2. Tip in the lavender, sift in the flour and gently combine with a spoon, then tip on to a lightly floured surface and gently knead until fully combined. Try to handle the dough as little as possible; the heat from your hands will liven up the butter in the dough and leave it greasy and hard to handle.

3. Flour a sheet of baking parchment and lay the dough on to it. Flour the dough, lay another sheet of baking parchment on top, and roll it out between the 2 sheets to a depth of about 8mm. You may have to turn the parchment over from time to time, so peel it off and re-lay it to stop kinks forming.

4. Cut out your chosen shapes. Re-roll the leftover dough and make more biscuits. Lay the biscuits on a baking tray or sheet lined with baking parchment and put in the fridge for 20 minutes to firm up.

5. Preheat the oven to 180°C/fan 160°C/gas 4 and bake for 20–25 minutes or until they are just beginning to get the slightest tinge of colour. Don't over-bake them!

6. Take out and transfer to a cooling rack with a palette knife. Make a cup of tea and get dunking.

Extras
Thick shortbread biscuits are absolutely perfect for dunking in tea or making as a gift. The salt and the lavender combined in this recipe make them really moreish, so be careful; your friends may get fewer than you had intended... Make sure you use lavender flowers, not lavender essence, or the shortbread will taste soapy. Try making them with different herbs or flavours: a bit of fresh lemon thyme works well; maybe try a bit of unwaxed lemon zest, too. As long as you roll them out gently and don't over-work the dough, you're good to go.

PEANUT BUTTER BUILDING SITE COOKIES

LEVEL 1

These are my dad's favourite. Whenever we're on a building site and it's his turn to go and get the biscuits, he always comes back with these. I learned to make them years ago, mainly just to have some in reserve for when we couldn't find a shop that sold them. These days I still can't seem to make enough and my daughters are now hooked on them, too. It looks as though three generations of Burrs will be dunking for just a bit too long and fishing these out of the bottom of a cuppa. You can too, if you like.

MAKES 40

Ingredients

120g unsalted butter, at room
    temperature
120g crunchy peanut butter
120g caster sugar
120g light soft brown sugar
    (don't be tempted to use
    dark brown; it makes
    them sink)
1 large egg
½ tsp vanilla bean paste
100g plain flour
1 tsp baking powder
½ tsp table salt
120g porridge oats
50g unsalted peanuts

Tool Kit

3 baking trays or sheets
electric whisk
wire cooling rack
palette knife

1. Preheat the oven to 200°C/fan 180°C/gas 6 and line 3 baking trays or sheets with baking parchment.

2. Beat together the butter, peanut butter and the sugars with an electric whisk until smooth and light-coloured. Beat in the egg and vanilla bean paste.

3. In a separate bowl, sift together the flour, baking powder and salt, mix in the oats, then fold them into the wet mixture, mixing well with a wooden spoon.

4. Take teaspoon-sized blobs of mixture and shape them into rough balls using 2 spoons. (If you use your fingers, the butter will melt and you'll end up with a sticky mess.) Load all the baking trays with blobs of mixture, leaving plenty of space for the cookies to spread out.

5. Stick 2–3 peanut halves into the top of each blob of mix, neaten them up with your fingers and bake for 10–12 minutes or until golden brown.

6. Take out and allow to stand for 5 minutes before transferring to a cooling rack with a palette knife. They will still be soft at this stage, so be gentle with them. Eat the lot, then go back to step 1.

Extras

These are excellent as they are, but if you feel like mucking around with them I can highly recommend making chocolate peanut butter cookies, either by spreading them with melted chocolate or adding chocolate chips to the dough.

FENNEL SEEDED THINS

I can make massive cakes with multiple layers covered in fruit, meringue and honeycomb, but it's always these thins my wife asks for. It's not hard to see why; these can be dangerously moreish and – if you don't pay attention – you will barely notice yourself inhaling a batch. To allow for this, I've gauged this recipe to make two batches, so you can bake one, scoff the lot, and still have another batch ready to cook, just waiting in the fridge… It is difficult to roll these out as thinly as you need and they can be fiddly to handle, so a little perseverance is needed.

MAKES 2 BATCHES OF AROUND 40 EACH

Ingredients

250g plain flour
1 tsp baking powder
½ tsp table salt
¼ tsp freshly ground
    black pepper
2 tsp fennel seeds
2 tsp sesame seeds
2 tsp poppy seeds
60g unsalted butter, chilled

Tool Kit

rolling pin
6cm fluted round cutter
    (or any other cutter of
    your choice)
2 baking trays
wire cooling rack
palette knife

1. Sift the flour, baking powder and salt into a bowl, then stir in the pepper and all the seeds. Cut the butter into small cubes and rub into the dry mixture until it resembles breadcrumbs.

2. Pour 100ml of cold water into the bowl and mix with a wooden spoon until dry enough to handle, then continue to lightly knead with your hands in the bowl until the mixture becomes smooth. Be careful not to over-work the dough, as this will develop the gluten and stop the biscuits from having a snap when you break them. Cut the ball of dough in half, wrap half in cling film and stick it in the fridge; it will last in there for 3–4 days.

3. Take the remaining dough and cut it in half again. Roll out each piece between 2 sheets of baking parchment until the dough is 1–2mm thick. You'll need to turn the sheets over regularly while rolling out, to take out the kinks that will form in the paper.

4. Using a 6cm fluted round cutter, press out around 40 biscuits. You'll need to press quite hard to cut through the seeds, but it will work. When pulling the excess dough away from the cut-out biscuits, use quick, sharp movements, so the biscuits don't stretch out of shape.

5. Lay the biscuits on 2 baking trays lined with baking parchment. Once on the baking trays, prick each biscuit with a fork to stop them bubbling up in the oven, then put in the fridge for 30 minutes.

6. Preheat the oven to 180°C/fan 160°C/gas 4 and bake the biscuits for 20–22 minutes. Keep an eye on them towards the end, as they can overcook very quickly, being so thin. Take out and transfer to a cooling rack with a palette knife. Eat with cheese and chutney.

Extras

I really like the strong fennel taste in these biscuits. The poppy and sesame seeds end up working as a texture, with their flavour being blown away by the fennel. Feel free to go mad in your herb cupboard and combine whatever flavours you can find. My wife really likes rosemary and chilli. For me, thins are a perfect opportunity to shift more cheese into the house, so it's a win-win.

LEMON CURD SANDWICH BISCUITS

When I was a kid, my mum would make lemon curd for one weekend every year. And she would make loads! I'm not sure who it was for or even where it went but, for me, the destination wasn't important. The whole house would smell of lemons, and my sisters and I would get in trouble for nicking a jar or two to eat with a spoon in secret. Making these biscuits takes me back to those days, when the only thing we had to worry about was getting caught (but we always managed to eat at least one jar before she found us).

MAKES AROUND 12

Ingredients

90g unsalted butter, at
    room temperature
175g caster sugar, plus more
    to sprinkle
1 large egg
1 tsp vanilla bean paste
finely grated zest of
    1 unwaxed lemon
200g plain flour, plus more
    to dust
about ½ jar of lemon curd
    (or see page 142
    for home-made)

Tool Kit

electric whisk
rolling pin
2 baking sheets or trays
2 same shape but different-
    sized cookie cutters, about
    6cm and 2cm (I like to make
    these star-shaped)
wire cooling rack
palette knife

1. Beat the butter and sugar in a bowl with an electric whisk until light-coloured and smooth. (If the butter is not at room temperature, chop it up, put into a jug of tepid water for 10 minutes to soften up, then drain off the water.) Add the egg, vanilla bean paste and lemon zest and continue to beat until fully incorporated (you will need to scrape down the sides of the bowl).

2. Sift the flour into the mixture and gently mix it in with a wooden spoon until fully combined, then shape into a ball by hand.

3. Roll out on to a floured sheet of baking parchment to around 5mm thick. Slide the parchment on to a baking sheet or tray and put it into the fridge for 10 minutes to firm up.

4. Remove from the fridge and press out your biscuit shapes using a 6cm cutter. You will need 12 bases and 12 tops with holes cut out of them using 2cm cutters. Combine the offcuts and re-roll them on a floured work surface. Try to be fairly quick doing this, as the mixture will warm up and get sticky. (If it does, just pop it back in the fridge to firm up again.)

5. Arrange the shapes on 2 baking sheets or trays lined with baking parchment and cool in the fridge for another 20 minutes.

6. Preheat the oven to 190°C/fan 170°C/gas 5 and bake the biscuits for 7 minutes, then take both trays out. Sprinkle the 'top' biscuits (the ones with the holes) with caster sugar, then return both trays to the oven and cook for a further 5 minutes or until golden brown. Take out and transfer to a cooling rack with a palette knife. Allow to cool fully.

7. Assemble by spreading the lemon curd on the bottom biscuits and sandwiching the tops on.

Extras

These lemon vanilla biscuits are nice with or without lemon curd in the middle. Sometimes I like to swap a lime into the biscuit mixture, or into the curd, but remember that 1 lemon usually equates to about 2½ limes. Citrus curds are always good to make and store for a few weeks in sterilised jars (see page 211) in the fridge... if they last that long. You can also replace the curd with thick blueberry jam for a really good combo.

CHOCOLATE ORANGE BISCOTTI DUNKERS

Biscotti are one of my favourite biscuits to dunk. As a builder, I've spent a considerable amount of time researching biscuits for dunking and this is right up there. When I first started going out with my wife, she used to come and see me on building sites every now and again and laugh at me and my builder mates bellowing, 'Oi! Who's nicked all my biscotti?' Not what you expect to hear shouted from the top of a scaffold...

MAKES 20–25
Ingredients
2 large eggs
200g caster sugar
finely grated zest of 1 orange
100g whole pistachios, shelled
    and chopped
50g chocolate chips
50g cocoa powder
200g plain flour, plus more
    to dust
1 tsp baking powder

Tool Kit
baking tray or sheet
electric whisk

1. Preheat the oven to 180°C/fan 160°C/gas 4 and lay baking parchment on a baking tray or sheet.

2. In a bowl, whisk together the eggs and sugar with an electric whisk until light-coloured and smooth. Fold in the orange zest, pistachios and chocolate chips.

3. Sift together the cocoa powder, flour and baking powder, then fold into the wet mixture. This mixture will be quite dense, but still sticky.

4. Turn out on to a floured worksurface and divide into 2 equal halves. Roll each half with your hands into a sausage about 25cm long and lay it on the prepared baking tray, spaced at least 5cm apart.

5. Bake for 35 minutes, then allow to cool for 15 minutes.

6. When cool enough to handle, slice each log diagonally with a very sharp knife into 1cm slices and return to the oven for 10 minutes to dry out.

7. Take out and allow to cool. These biscuits can be stored for about a fortnight in an airtight container (if they last that long).

Extras
The thing that makes biscotti is the double baking. This dries the biscuits out and allows them to absorb plenty of coffee when dunked.

They work really well with whole nuts in them; try hazelnuts, walnuts, almonds or pecans.

You can put dried fruits in them (I really love a sour cherry in biscotti).

Don't feel obliged to make chocolate versions; you can always replace the cocoa powder with flour and incorporate spices to zing them up a bit.

But make sure you dip them in strong coffee when you do bake them and take a good 15 minutes out of your day to just sit and enjoy.

BLACKCURRANT MACARONS

A delicious treat. I never had a macaron as a child, as I don't think they were popular in this country back then. But now I can make them, there's no looking back. They're not difficult to do once you've got the knack. I avoided them for ages, thinking they'd be too hard, but was surprised by how straightforward they are. And you can modify them in loads of fun ways.

MAKES 20
Ingredients
For the shells
3 large egg whites
30g caster sugar
1 tsp vanilla bean paste
purple gel food colour
210g icing sugar
150g ground almonds

For the filling
100g mascarpone
75g double cream
100g icing sugar
2 tbsp crème de cassis

Tool Kit
electric whisk
2 piping bags
4cm round cutter (optional)
2 baking sheets or trays

1. To make the shells, first whisk the egg whites with the caster sugar and vanilla bean paste, using an electric whisk, until very soft peaks form. Add the food colour and whisk until stiff peaks form; these look good with a strong colour, but add as much as you like. (Gel colours won't alter the texture of the mixture too much.)

2. In a separate bowl, sift the icing sugar and mix in the ground almonds. Fold in the whisked egg a couple of spoonfuls at a time. Once the mixture is smooth, load it into a piping bag and set aside.

3. Prepare 2 sheets of baking parchment by drawing around a 4cm round cutter, or similar-sized template, to give a guide for piping. Draw 20 circles on each sheet, with the circles at least 2cm apart. Turn the baking parchment over and put each on to a baking sheet or tray, so the pencil markings are on the bottom side, but still visible.

4. Pipe the mixture on to the parchment, within the circles. Try to keep the piping bag as still as possible when piping and to leave a single dimple in the centre of each blob as you pull the piping bag off.

5. Firmly slam each baking tray on to a worktop a few times to flatten the dimples caused by the piping, and set aside for 45–60 minutes.

6. Preheat the oven to 150°C/fan 130°C/gas 2. Bake for 18–20 minutes. Leave to cool completely before peeling away the baking parchment.

7. Make the filling by beating the mascarpone and cream together with the electric whisk until fully combined. Add the icing sugar and beat together until the mixture just begins to thicken. Add the cassis and continue beating until thickened, then load into a piping bag.

8. Pipe the filling on to a shell, then gently pop on another shell. Be careful when pressing the top shell on, as they are fragile. Repeat until all the macarons are sandwiched together.

Extras

Once you have got the hang of making the shells, you can flavour them in any way you want. The choices are endless, so experiment away…

For the shells, try replacing one-quarter of the almonds with ground pistachios.

Sprinkle the shells with desiccated coconut before cooking.

Make flavoured creams using different liqueurs or other flavourings.

BUILDING A CABIN IN THE WOODS

From the smallest gingerbread house to a scale model of the Palace of Versailles, gingerbread construction has always fascinated me. It's probably the builder in me, as I love to make higher and higher biscuit constructions. Here I'm going to show you how to make a woodland scene. We'll look at glueing biscuits together, sliding them together as interlocking pieces and making melted sugar glass for windows. This will give you a few ideas to think about and hopefully muck about with to make your own amazing biscuit masterpieces.

FEEDS A CROWD

Ingredients

For the gingerbread

900g plain flour, plus more
    to dust
5 tsp ground ginger
2 tsp mixed spice
4 tsp bicarbonate of soda
230g unsalted butter
200g golden syrup
230g light brown
    muscovado sugar
2 large eggs
a bag of boiled sweets
mixed sweets, to
    decorate (optional)

For the royal icing

3 large egg whites or 6 tbsp
    Two Chicks liquid
    egg white
1 tbsp lemon juice
500g icing sugar, plus more to
    dust (optional)
gel food colours

Tool Kit

3 baking sheets or trays
rolling pin
food processor (optional)
palette knife
electric whisk
small piping bags
2mm icing nozzle
display board

1. Trace the templates (see opposite) on to thin card, such as an empty cereal box, then cut them out. Preheat the oven to 170°C/fan 150°C/gas 3½ and line 3 baking sheets or trays with baking parchment.

2. Make the gingerbread in 2 batches, cooking the first batch before making the second, or it will cool down and be much harder to roll out and shape. You probably won't get all the templates you need cut out of the first batch, though it depends how economical you are with your cutting. Sift half the flour, spices and bicarbonate of soda into a bowl and mix thoroughly with a wooden spoon.

3. Melt half the butter, syrup and sugar in a saucepan over a low heat. (To get an accurate measurement of golden syrup, put the saucepan on your scales and set them to zero, then pour in the sticky stuff.) Pour it into the bowl with the flour and mix with a wooden spoon for 30 seconds to distribute the heat. This doesn't have to be fully mixed, you're just doing it so the egg doesn't cook in the hot sugar. Break in 1 egg and continue mixing until the dough is fully combined.

4. Tear off about one third of the dough and roll out on a floured work surface to about 3mm thick (about the depth of a pound coin). I have been doing this by eye for years, but I recently got a rolling pin with depth guides as a present. If you can get one, they're excellent.

5. Lay your templates on the dough and cut out with a sharp knife; I use a long knife and cut straight down for edges; a small knife for curves.

6. There are 3 templates opposite for the house, but remember to cut out 2 of each: 2 pieces for the roof, 2 pieces for the front and back, and 2 pieces for the sides. Don't forget to cut the open doorway into the front of the house only and the windows into both the sides.

7. Gently pick up the gingerbread pieces and lay on the prepared baking sheets or trays, then lay the templates back over each piece to make sure you haven't stretched or bent the dough (if you have, reshape it on a baking sheet). Re-roll the offcuts and remaining dough to make more templates.

8. To make the glass for the windows, take 1 colour of the boiled sweets and blitz them down to dust in a food processor (it must be absolutely dry when doing this, or you'll get a sticky gunge, rather

Continued...

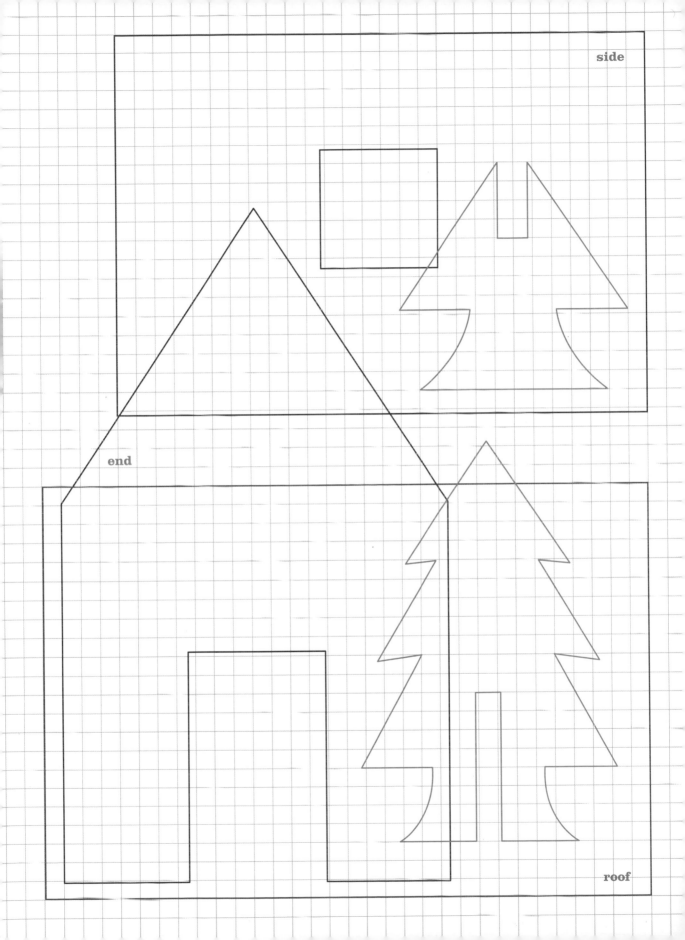

side

end

roof

than fine dust). If you mix different-coloured sweets, it turns into quite a sludgy colour. If you don't have a food processor, put them in a freezer bag and bash them with your rolling pin. Put 1 tsp of the coloured sugar dust in the window hole on your biscuits.

9. Bake the gingerbread for 9 minutes. Take each tray out at a time, lay the templates over each biscuit and cut off any edges which have warped during cooking. Bake for another 9 minutes to fully cook.

10. Take out of the oven. Leave to cool on the baking trays for 10 minutes to allow the gingerbread to firm up and the sugar to set.

11. Lift the gingerbread off the baking trays. You will need to slide a palette knife underneath the windows to make sure they don't stick to the baking parchment.

12. Follow steps 2–3 to make the second batch of gingerbread dough.

13. Next make some trees, using the tree templates. Feel free to make your own if you want variety in your woodland; the important thing to get right is the interlocking notches that you're going to shape. These can also be used to make characters (people, animals and so on) that are free-standing, so populate your forest as you see fit!

14. Roll out the gingerbread in batches, cut it out and lay on the baking sheets or trays as described above. Bake for 9 minutes as before, then be really careful when cutting to the template, as the width of the notches in the stands is the most important factor in making interlocking shapes. Return to the oven and bake for the remaining 9 minutes. After taking out for the final time, use the templates to check the notches again. If they're too small, you can still saw away at them with a serrated knife to make them bigger, but be careful as the gingerbread gets more brittle the cooler it becomes. Leave to cool.

15. Make the royal icing by mixing the egg whites and lemon juice in a large bowl, then gradually beat in the icing sugar with an electric whisk on a slow speed, a couple of spoonfuls at a time. Once all the sugar is incorporated, turn the electric whisk up to full speed and beat until the icing becomes firmer. Load some of the icing into a small piping bag fitted with a 2mm nozzle and put the rest of the icing in an airtight container in the fridge.

16. To build the house, take the back of the house (the end without a doorway) and pipe a thick line of icing along the bottom, to stick it to the display board. Pipe icing along each of the sides and along the bottom of the side walls and glue the 2 side walls to the back of the house. Take the front of the house, pipe icing on the bottom and on each of the sides and stick this to the 2 sides on the display board. You can use tins or books or whatever you like to prop your walls in position until the icing dries, about 30 minutes should do the trick.

17. Once the walls have set in place, pipe icing on to their top edges and along the top of the roof pieces and lay the roof in place. You'll need to prop up the roof to stop it sliding down while it dries. Or you can hold it in place for a few minutes. Once the structure of your house is stable, use some remaining plain royal icing to fill in any holes around the edges and to further anchor your house to the board.

18. To start decorating the trees, take about one-fifth of the icing from the airtight container and mix thoroughly with some green gel colour to make a rich green, then load into a small piping bag fitted with the 2mm nozzle. Pipe outlines of the foliage and the impression of leaves; you don't need an accurate representation – the effect will be better if you work quickly and don't worry about precision.

19. Mix up other colours as you need them and try to use all of each colour before you move on to the next; this takes forethought, but is worth it as the icing can dry in the nozzle and be a pain to get running again. If you are having trouble with a dry nozzle, dip the tip in water for 30 seconds to dissolve the icing, then have another go.

20. Once all the icing decoration has been applied and is dry, you can assemble the interlocking elements of your scene around your decorated forest cabin (see overleaf). I tile the roof with chocolate buttons, and the kids stick dolly mixtures over every available surface. If you're feeling Christmassy, give the scene a dust of icing sugar (great for hiding imperfections) and use as a lovely centrepiece.

Extras

So, that's gingerbread worked out; what about some other biscuits to build with? Peanut butter cookies (see page 94) make excellent desert islands and you can stick other biscuit constructions in them while they are still warm and malleable, as this helps the more precarious free-standing things to stand up. The same recipe makes excellent stepping stones for woodland scenes...

Vanilla biscuits (see page 96) work well, but I'd be wary of making anything too big or elaborate with them as they are not as hard, so stick to simple characters (preferably short ones!). Try brandy snaps as tree trunks; they set hard and can be moulded into curves for towers or tunnels.

My wife has thrown a gingerbread house-decorating party at Christmas for her mates and their kids. For this, make scaled-down versions of this template with no windows. Fill a table with squeezy icing bottles and bowls of sweets. It's a great party idea if you have children with December birthdays, though I think the grown-ups enjoy it more than the kids!

The most important thing to remember is to eat them! Don't leave them to go soft as you admire them. Make them, show them off, take a picture, then play King Kong vs. Godzilla with the kids and destroy them; it really is half the fun!

6

SAVOURY PIES

LEFTOVER CHICKEN PIE

In our house, a chicken gets three goes: roasted on day one, turned into a pie on day two, and as chicken and vegetable soup on day three. This recipe is probably the closest thing I've got to a 'signature bake' and it's the dinner that friends and family request the most. It's really economical and we look forward to it more than we do the Sunday roast the day before. Absolutely delicious on a cold Monday evening!

SERVES 4–6

Ingredients

For the shortcrust pastry

300g plain flour, plus more
    to dust
½ tsp table salt
75g unsalted butter, chilled
    and chopped
75g lard, chilled and chopped
1 large egg, lightly beaten

For the filling

100g smoked streaky
    bacon, chopped
2 tsp sunflower oil
1 medium onion, chopped
1 leek, sliced about 5mm thick
400ml chicken stock, or
    leftover gravy if you have it
2 carrots, chopped
4 leftover roast
    potatoes, chopped
200g cold roast chicken,
    ideally dark meat, chopped
1 tbsp dried Italian
    mixed herbs
2 bay leaves
1 tbsp unsalted butter
3 tsp plain flour
60ml milk
30g frozen peas
sea salt and freshly ground
    black pepper

1. First make the pastry. Put the flour and salt in a bowl, add the butter and lard and rub together until the mixture looks like breadcrumbs. Gradually add up to 4 tbsp of cold water, continuing to mix by hand until the dough starts to come together. Cut the dough in half. Shape each half lightly into a ball, flatten to a disc of around 15cm, separately wrap in cling film and refrigerate for 30 minutes.

2. Lightly fry the bacon in the oil in a large pan. Add the onion and continue to fry until it softens and turns translucent. Add the leek and cook until it wilts. Pour in the stock or gravy. Add the carrots, potatoes and chicken with the herbs and bay leaves. Bring to the boil, then reduce the heat and simmer gently for 10–20 minutes, until the mixture has reduced a little.

3. In a small saucepan, mix the butter and flour over a low heat until it forms a paste, add the milk and mix to a smooth paste. Stir the paste and the peas into the chicken mixture, season with salt and pepper to taste and heat through, stirring occasionally, for about 5 minutes. Leave to cool. Preheat the oven to 220°C/fan 200°C/gas 7.

4. Take the cold pastry out of the fridge and roll one half of it out on a floured work surface to a circle about 25cm in diameter. Roll the pastry up on the rolling pin, then lay into a 22cm shallow pie tin, using your fingers to gently push it into the dish. Pour in the cold filling: be careful – you don't want to get any on the rim of pastry or you won't get it to seal and your filling will leak out. Brush the pie rim with plenty of beaten egg.

5. Roll out the second disc of pastry to about 25cm in diameter. Lay it on top of the pie and trim off the excess with a knife. Crimp the top and bottom layers together either with your fingers or by pressing down with the back of a fork. Roll together the pastry offcuts and cut out leaf shapes (or any other shape) to decorate the pie. Stick these bits to the pie with a little egg, then brush the top of the pie with more egg. Make a few slashes in the pastry to allow steam to escape.

6. Bake for about 25 minutes, or until golden brown. Serve hot and try not to fight over who gets seconds.

Tool Kit

rolling pin

22cm shallow pie tin

pastry brush

Extras

'Leftover' pies are one of those things that everyone should learn how to make. Whatever you've got lying about in the fridge can go in: a bit of ham, some scraps from a leg of lamb. My usual method is to work back from what the original meal was and stick it into a pie (which is why I think a few leftover roast potatoes in there are lovely). If you have any leftover gravy, be aware that it will be quite salty, so taste as you go. I've done this recipe with Italian mixed herbs, but only because we've always got them lying around. Try a few tsp of fresh thyme and 2 tbsp of lemon juice instead to put a bit of zing into the mix. Make these loads, though, and the next day, boil up that chicken carcass and make soup.

STEAK AND ALE PIE

LEVEL 2

This is Desperate Dan territory. Making massive pies out of hot water crust pastry is always a good thing to do on a cold day. They're warming and hearty and they set you up. I've been baking this recipe for years; in fact it has been fun to try and work out exactly *how* I do it for this book, as I've been making it on autopilot for so long. If you're going to have a go at this – and I really hope you do – get the best-quality beef you can afford. Look for a marbled effect on the meat and cut away any gristle; it will really make the difference.

SERVES 6–8

Ingredients

For the filling

5 tbsp plain flour

2 tsp sea salt flakes and 1 tsp freshly ground black pepper

1kg Aberdeen Angus braising beef, chopped

25g salted butter

a little vegetable oil

500ml bottle of strong ale (I use Old Speckled Hen)

3 large red onions, chopped

5 carrots, chopped

500ml strong beef stock (made with 2 stock cubes)

2 tbsp Worcestershire sauce

1 tbsp brown sugar

5 bay leaves

2 tsp thyme leaves

300g mushrooms, chopped

3 garlic cloves, crushed

3 tbsp lemon juice

For the hot water crust

250ml water

100g lard

10g table salt

450g plain flour, plus more to dust

1 large egg, lightly beaten

1. For the filling, put the flour in a bowl and mix it with the sea salt and pepper. Roll the beef in the seasoned flour to coat.

2. In a large pan, melt the butter with some oil and fry the beef in a few batches over a high heat until well browned. Set the browned beef aside while you fry the rest. Pour one-quarter of the beer into the pan and reduce the heat to low. Swirl the beer around in the pan and scrape the base to release any of the flour and meat juices that have stuck. Pour this into the bowl with the beef.

3. Pour a little more oil into the empty pan and fry the onions and carrots over a medium heat, stirring occasionally. Add the rest of the beer, the stock, Worcestershire sauce, brown sugar, bay leaves and thyme. Bring to a simmer and leave to reduce for 1 hour, remembering to stir regularly. Stir in the mushrooms, garlic and lemon juice and cook for another 30 minutes. You may need to add a little water if the filling seems a little dry (use your judgement). Leave to cool completely.

4. Preheat the oven to 220°C/fan 200°C/gas 7. For the pastry, put the water, lard and salt in a small saucepan and set over a medium heat. Put the flour into a large bowl and, once the water and lard are boiling, pour them over the flour, stirring with a wooden spoon until the dough has come together, then tip out on to a floured work surface and knead for 2–3 minutes. Return to the bowl and lay a tea towel over it to keep the heat in. You need to work quickly now, for if the pastry cools down too much it will be difficult to shape.

Continued on page 114...

Tool Kit
rolling pin
23cm springform cake tin
pastry brush

5. Take about two-thirds of the dough and roll out on a floured surface to a circle 28–30cm in diameter. Roll this on to a rolling pin and lay inside a 23cm springform cake tin. Use your fingers to mould the pastry into the tin, making sure you work it into the corners. Allow the excess to flop over the edge (this will help prevent the pastry from falling into the tin). Plug any holes with more pastry and ladle in the cold filling, making sure not to slop any down the sides of the pastry.

6. Brush the inner exposed rim of the pastry with plenty of beaten egg, then roll out the remaining pastry on a floured surface to a circle of around 28cm in diameter. Roll this on to the rolling pin and lay out on the pie. Use your fingers to work the pie top into position, making a good seal between the two layers of pastry. Use two fingers and a thumb to crimp the pastry closed, then brush liberally with beaten egg (reserve the remaining egg). Slash three holes in the top of the pie to allow steam to escape.

7. Bake for 45 minutes, then release the springform sides – the pastry will be cooked enough to hold its shape now – brush the sides of the pie with more egg and return to the oven for a final 20 minutes until the pie is a rich brown colour. If the top begins to brown too much, cover it with a layer of foil. Serve hot with roast potatoes and peas.

Extras

I could eat pie every day with no complaints whatsoever. This recipe is delicious and a good excuse to sneak some good ale into the house. The pie is relatively easy to scale up or down depending on what size tins you have, as you can make as much or as little pastry as you like. If I have a bit left over, I usually knock up a hand-raised pie (see page 118). Make chicken and mushroom pie in the same way, but roast the chicken first and use dried wild mushrooms, as they offer a really intense flavour. The main advice I would give is to keep practising and make loads of pies. They're such a good dinner and really worth the effort. You can get some really interesting-shaped pie tins, too, so have fun and experiment.

SEA-FISHERMAN'S PIE

LEVEL 2

I go sea-fishing whenever I get the chance; I have done for years. I usually go with my dad and try to bring a few mates along, too. A side effect of this is a freezer full of fish, so I developed this recipe to use it all up. If you somehow manage not to go fishing every month (you're missing out), then this recipe works really well with the packs of mixed fish you can buy in the supermarket. It's not complicated to make puff pastry, just a bit long-winded, so be brave and have a go.

SERVES 4–6

Ingredients

For the puff pastry

225g strong white bread flour, plus more to dust

½ tsp table salt

225g unsalted butter, chilled

1 tsp lemon juice

1 large egg, lightly beaten

For the filling

4 spring onions, chopped

a little olive oil

30g unsalted butter

2 tbsp plain flour

250ml whole milk

50ml dry white wine

75g Cheddar cheese, grated

1 tsp Dijon mustard

2 garlic cloves, crushed

25g chives, chopped

75g frozen peas

75g frozen sweetcorn

300g chopped mixed fish (salmon, haddock, and cod or pollack)

100g raw shelled prawns

sea salt and black pepper

Tool Kit

rolling pin

tape measure (optional, but I find it really useful)

23 x 18cm rectangular (or 23cm round) deep-sided pie dish with rim

pastry brush

1. This is very important (and a bit like a choose-your-own-adventure): if you don't have a day to prepare, just buy a pack of all-butter puff pastry from the shops and move straight to step 6. If you do have a day to prepare, move to step 2.

2. To make the puff pastry, first mix the flour and salt in a large bowl, then chop 25g of the butter and rub into the flour with your fingers. Add the lemon juice and 140ml of cold water and mix with a knife until the mixture is brought together enough to handle. Tip out on to a floured work surface and knead until smooth and elastic (probably 5–10 minutes). Allow the dough to rest for 5 minutes.

3. Roll out on a floured surface to a rectangle of 51 x 17cm (or thereabouts). You need quite a bit of worktop space for this. Roll out the remaining 200g butter between sheets of cling film to a rectangle of 33 x 15cm. You'll need to peel off and reapply the cling film regularly to stop it ripping. Working quickly now, peel the top layer of cling film off the butter and flip the butter on to the rolled-out dough, covering two-thirds of the length of the dough and also leaving a clear rim around all the edges. Fold the unbuttered dough on to half of the butter and press the edges to seal the butter in. Fold this layer over to cover the remaining butter and press down the edges all round to form a 17cm square: 2 layers of butter separated by 3 layers of dough. Wrap in cling film and chill in the fridge for 30 minutes.

4. Take out of the fridge and roll back out to about 51 x 17cm. Fold up into thirds as before, to make a square. Turn the square through 90 degrees and roll out to 51 x 17cm again, then fold up as before. Wrap in cling film and chill for another 30 minutes.

5. Repeat the last step, so the pastry has been folded a total of 5 times. Chill for another 30 minutes.

6. Meanwhile, make the filling. Fry the spring onions in the olive oil in a large pan over a medium heat for 2–3 minutes. Set aside. Melt the butter in the same pan and stir in the flour to form a thick paste. Gradually add the milk, about 50ml at a time, whisking well between each addition. (If you add it all at once, you'll have a lumpy sauce.) Whisk in the wine, then stir in the cheese, mustard and garlic. Allow

Continued...

to cook for a couple of minutes, remembering to make sure the sauce doesn't dry on the sides of the pan. Add the spring onions, chopped chives, peas and sweetcorn and cook for another 2–3 minutes. Add the fish and prawns and cook for another 5 minutes, then season with salt and pepper and scrape the filling into a 23 x 18cm rectangular (or 23cm round) deep-sided pie dish with a rim. Leave to cool.

7. Preheat the oven to 240°C/fan 220°C/gas 9. Roll out the puff pastry on a floured work surface to a square of roughly 30cm and cut off enough 3cm-wide strips to lay around the rim of the dish. These stop the puff crust from shrinking back too much while cooking. Use plenty of beaten egg to stick these strips around the edge, then brush their tops with more egg. Roll up the remaining pastry on to a rolling pin and lay on top of the pie dish, pressing the top layer of puff down on to the strips, then cut off the excess.

8. Gently use a sharp knife to cut small grooves along the side edges of the pastry to expose some of the puff layers. This allows the pastry to puff up more easily when cooking.

9. Paint with beaten egg and bake in the oven for 20–25 minutes until golden brown. Serve piping hot with new potatoes and green beans.

Extras

One of the good things about fish pie is that if it swims, and you can get the bones out, it can go in the pie. The ingredients I've chosen are readily available from the supermarket, but if you're lucky enough to be or know a fisherman, use whatever you can lay your hands on. The puff top is a really good touch, but if you don't have the time to make it or there's none in the shop, you can top with mashed potato and it will still be delicious. Incorporate other flavours such as dill and capers into the filling and add a couple of tbsp of lemon juice, too, if you like. Put shellfish in if you want them: a few mussels or cockles can add great texture and flavour. Oh, and take up sea-fishing, because it's ace.

INDIVIDUAL PORK PIES

LEVEL 3

Who doesn't love a pork pie? OK, some of you might not, but you'll have to bear with the rest of us, because there are days when I'd frankly crawl over broken glass to get one. While I can easily inhale as many supermarket pork pies as you can throw at me, there's nothing quite like a pie you've made yourself. You can put in plenty of flavouring, loads of different-flavoured jelly (sorry, jelly haters – it's an essential part of pork pie preservation, so get used to it) and you can show off about how clever you are.

MAKES 4

Ingredients

For the hot water crust

1 quantity Hot Water Crust dough (see page 112), fresh-made

a little plain flour, to dust

1 large egg, lightly beaten

For the filling

150g sausagemeat

150g smoked bacon, chopped into 5mm pieces

200g pork belly, chopped into 5mm bits (or minced pork)

1 tsp sea salt and ¼ tsp freshly ground black pepper

¼ tsp cayenne pepper

1 small onion, finely chopped

5 sage leaves, finely chopped

2 tbsp finely chopped parsley

1 tsp thyme leaves

For the jelly

1 gelatine leaf

½ tsp vegetable bouillon (or chicken stock cube)

Tool Kit

rolling pin

empty, clean jam jar

string

pastry brush

wire cooling rack

large piping bag nozzle, or very small funnel

1. Pop the hot water crust dough into a bowl, cover with a tea towel (to keep it warm) and leave to relax while you prepare the filling.

2. For the filling, mix the sausagemeat in a bowl with the bacon and pork belly. Add the salt, pepper and cayenne. Sprinkle over the onion and herbs, then mix everything together.

3. Cut the pastry into quarters, return 3 of them to the bowl and cover with a tea towel again to keep them warm and malleable. Take the first ball of pastry and tear off one-quarter of it for a lid. Roll out the remaining pastry on a floured work surface into a disc of roughly 15cm. Lay this over the base of an upside-down, clean jam jar and work the dough round it to form a cup 8–10cm high. Wrap a strip of baking parchment around the pastry and tie with some string, then turn the jar up so the pastry is sitting on the work surface. Half-fill the jar with hot water and start to tease the pastry case off the jar. (The hot water re-melts the lard in the pastry and allows it to slip off.) You will get a bit of suction between the jar and the pastry when doing this, but once the pastry is released you can poke it all back into place (see photographs on page 120).

4. As soon as you have released the pie cup, load it with filling. About 2–3 tbsp, pressed down, should do the trick to bring it to about 1cm from the top of the pastry.

5. Roll out the pastry for the top, on a lightly floured surface, to about 1cm wider than the top and pinch into place with your fingers and thumb. If your pastry has sunk down lower than the baking parchment at this stage, just cut some paper away to make this crimping easier. Poke a small hole with a sharp knife into the top of the pie to allow steam to escape and for filling with jelly later. Make the other pies in the same way and leave them all in the fridge for 30 minutes for the pastry to firm up. Preheat the oven to 180°C/fan 160°C/gas 4.

6. Take the pies out of the fridge and cut off the string and baking parchment. Brush each pie all over with the egg and bake in the oven for 30 minutes. Take the pies out and brush with more egg, then bake for another 30–45 minutes until they are a nice rich brown colour. Check them after 30 minutes and, if the pies still look a bit anaemic, brush them all with more egg and whack them back in.

Continued...

7. When the pies are cooked, take them out of the oven and set on a cooling rack. Meanwhile, make the jelly. Cut the gelatine leaf into squares of about 2cm and mix into 125ml of boiling water in a measuring jug. Stir in the bouillon or stock cube and set aside.

8. Once the pies are cold, pour the jelly in through the holes in the tops, using a large piping bag nozzle or a funnel to help. Leave them for 1–2 hours to fully cool down, then pop in the fridge for a couple of hours or overnight for the jelly to set.

Extras

Once you have got the hang of making and shaping hot water crust, it opens up a whole new branch of baking for you. It is very easy to scale up or down if you have different-sized tins and want to make massive pork pies. Remember, though: if you are making a big one, cook for 1½–2 hours – it is a solid block of meat after all! I really love this recipe, but feel free to muck about with the balance of herbs; traditional pork pies incorporate other fun stuff such as nutmeg and mace, so don't be afraid to experiment. It is quite important to maintain the proportions of the meats, though, as they each serve a role: belly for texture; bacon for salt; sausagemeat for structure. Have fun with this, as it's a bake you'll always want to come back to.

EXPEDITION PIE

I prefer the idea of an 'expedition' pie to a 'picnic' one. These pies hold together and incorporate loads of different flavours for when you're out and about with the kids. I love making the sharp layers you see when you cut into them. This flavour combination is one of my favourites.

SERVES 6–8

Ingredients

For the filling

300g skinless and boneless chicken breasts, chopped into 2cm cubes

sea salt and freshly ground black pepper

a little olive oil

75g green pesto

1 large red onion, peeled

1 red pepper

150g butternut squash, peeled

8 rashers of streaky bacon

75g feta cheese

50g walnuts

For the hot water crust

1 quantity Hot Water Crust dough (see page 112), fresh-made

plain flour, to dust

1 large egg, lightly beaten

For the jelly

3 gelatine leaves

½ chicken stock cube

Tool Kit

2 baking trays

rolling pin

900g loaf tin

pastry brush

wire cooling rack

1. For the filling, season the chicken with salt and pepper and fry in olive oil over a medium heat until lightly golden. Toss it in the pesto and set aside to cool.

2. Preheat the oven to 200°C/fan 180°C/gas 6. Slice the vegetables: the onion into 5mm-thick crescents, the pepper into strips and the butternut squash into 1cm-thick chips, about 10cm long. Drizzle the vegetables with a little olive oil and lay out on 2 baking trays. Season with salt and pepper and roast for 25 minutes. Leave to cool.

3. Meanwhile, fry off the bacon in a little more oil, then set aside. Slice the feta into 5mm-thick slices and roughly chop the walnuts.

4. Pop the hot water crust dough into a bowl and cover with a tea towel (to keep it warm). Make 2 strips of foil, folded over a few times for strength, and lay them into a 900g loaf tin, crossing over (this will help you lift the pie out later).

5. Take two-thirds of the pastry and roll out on a lightly floured work surface into a rectangle around 40 x 25cm. Roll up on to a rolling pin and lay into the prepared tin. Use your fingers to gently work the pastry into the corners of the tin.

6. Start to fill the pastry up. Begin with the cooled chicken, firmly pressing it down into the bottom. Add the red pepper, laying them on top of the chicken. Now add the feta and the walnuts, remembering to keep the layers even and pressed down. Add the squash next, followed by the bacon. Top with the onions. Brush the top edge of the pastry with beaten egg.

7. To make the lattice top, first roll out the remaining pastry on a floured surface. Cut it into 2cm-wide strips: 4 that are the length of the loaf tin (about 25cm) and 7 that are its width (about 12cm).

8. Lay the long strips, evenly spaced apart by 5mm, on the work surface. Fold back 2 alternate long strips of pastry. Lay a short strip on the remaining strips, then fold the long strips back. Carry on in this manner, alternating which of the long strips are folded back, to build the lattice.

9. Very carefully roll the lattice on to a rolling pin and lay on top of the pie. Press down the edges, so that the egg 'glues' the top and bottom together. Cut the excess pastry off with a sharp knife and crimp the edges around the pie.

Continued...

10. Brush the lattice with more egg and bake for 50 minutes. Check during the last 10 minutes that the pastry isn't burning. If it is taking on too much colour, cover with some foil for the last bit.

11. Take the pie out of the oven and gently lift it out of the tin using the foil strips (do not tip the pie out, or any liquid in it will pour out of the lattice). Paint the newly exposed edges of pastry with egg and return to the oven for a final 5 minutes.

12. For the jelly, soak the gelatine leaves in cold water for 5 minutes. Make the stock in a jug, using 200ml of boiling water and the stock cube. Stir the softened gelatine leaves into the stock until they have fully dissolved.

13. Carefully take the pie out of the oven and place on a wire rack to cool. When cool, pour the jelly in through the lattice holes to fill the pie and allow to cool completely for at least 1 hour on the wire rack, then refrigerate the pie for a couple of hours or overnight until completely chilled.

Extras

You can fill these pies with anything. I really like to put pickles in: onions, beetroot or piccalilli. Lots of different roasted vegetables always work well. One of my basic rules of thumb is that, if you can find it on a buffet table, you can put it in your expedition pie. Stuffing tends to work a treat in these pies, too, as does pretty much all kinds of cheese. Layer cold cuts or bacon in, too.

7

SWEET PIES

PLUM PIE

My kids love the book *Each Peach Pear Plum* by Janet and Allan Ahlberg; we know it off by heart. The children began requesting plum pie as soon as they could talk, as a result of seeing the lovely cartoon pie at the end of that book. This pie is as simple and as old as the ingredients that go in it. My parents have plum trees in their garden and always seem to go on holiday around plum-harvesting time, so it's usually my job to pick them. This is a great way to use them up.

SERVES 6–8
Ingredients
For the pastry
350g plain flour, plus more
  to dust
½ tsp table salt
160g unsalted butter, chilled
  and chopped
1 egg, lightly beaten

For the filling
1.2kg plums, pitted and cut
  into eighths
3 tsp lemon juice
75g caster sugar, plus more
  to sprinkle
4 tbsp cornflour

Tool Kit
food processor (optional)
rolling pin
25cm round metal pie dish
pie bird (optional)
pastry brush

1. Put the flour and salt in a bowl, then rub in the butter until the mixture resembles breadcrumbs. (If you have a food processor, you can pulse the butter and flour together. This will keep it colder as the heat from your hands won't transfer to the mix. Be careful not to over-mix, though, as you don't want to develop the gluten in the flour.) Mix in up to 90ml of cold water, first with a spoon, then with your fingers once the mix comes together. (You can also do this in the processor, but don't over-mix.) Cut the pastry in half, press each into a disc to help it cool more quickly, wrap in cling film and chill in the fridge for 30–45 minutes.

2. Put the plums in a saucepan, splash with the lemon juice, then sprinkle over the sugar. Set over a medium-low heat to reduce the juices for 25–30 minutes. Mix the cornflour with 4 tbsp of water, stir this into the plums, then allow to cool. Preheat the oven to 190°C/fan 170°C/gas 5.

3. Once the pastry has chilled, unwrap a disc and roll out on a floured work surface into a 30cm circle. Roll up on to the rolling pin and unroll over a 25cm round metal pie dish, pressing it in gently. Place a pie bird in the centre, if you have one, then pour in the plums. Brush the edge of the pastry with beaten egg.

4. Roll out the other half of the pastry slightly larger than the top of the pie dish and cut a small hole in the middle for the pie bird to poke through. Roll up on the rolling pin and lay out over the pie, making sure the pie bird sticks through the hole. Press down the edges of the pie and cut off the excess. Crimp the edges with the back of a fork and slash 4 air holes around the pie bird. Brush liberally with egg. If you like, you can cut out leaf shapes from the offcuts and stick them on, brushing them with egg, too. Sprinkle with sugar.

5. Bake for 40–50 minutes, until golden brown. Eat with cream or custard (see page 137 for home-made).

Extras
You can put anything in a fruit pie. Well, as long as it's fruit. Scrump whatever you like and bung it in. Apple and blackberry is my go-to filling outside plum season (or raisins if blackberries aren't in season). It is important to use a metal dish, as this allows heat to transfer to the base and cook the pastry (avoiding soggy bottoms). You can add spices: try cinnamon, nutmeg, ginger or allspice.

MINCE PIES

It's usually about mid-November when you can legitimately start eating mince pies, so make the most of that limited window to bake as many as you can! I love them hot and slathered in brandy and double cream. If you want to make your own mincemeat, I urge you to try it (see page 211). It is dead easy, but you do tend to make quite a lot of it at a time. If you just want mince pies as soon as possible, buy a regular 400g jar of mincemeat instead. Get the kids involved, too; there's nothing like piling into produce you've made with excited children during the Christmas holidays.

MAKES 12

Ingredients

For the sweet
shortcrust pastry

200g plain flour, plus more
to dust

½ tsp table salt

100g caster sugar, plus
more to sprinkle

100g unsalted butter, chilled
and chopped, plus more for
the tin

2 large eggs

For the filling

1 quantity home-made
Mincemeat (see page 211)

OR use a 400g jar of good-
quality shop-bought
mincemeat

Tool Kit

12-hole muffin tin

9cm fluted round cutter

7cm star-shaped cutter or
other Christmassy shape

pastry brush

1. Make the sweet pastry by first mixing the flour, salt and sugar, then rubbing in the butter to make a breadcrumb consistency. Break 1 egg into the bowl and mix with a wooden spoon until a soft dough has formed. Tip on to a floured work surface and gently knead for a minute or so, then mould into a disc about 10cm wide, wrap in cling film and put in the fridge for 30 minutes to firm up.

2. Preheat the oven to 220°C/fan 200°C/gas 7 and butter a 12-hole muffin tin. Unwrap the pastry and gently roll out on a well-floured surface, turning it regularly so it doesn't stick to the surface or crack too much. Roll out to the thickness of a pound coin (about 3mm). Use a 9cm fluted round cutter to cut out 12 discs and place each one in the muffin tin. Use your fingers to gently press the pastry into the shape of the tin, avoiding pressing down on the crinkled edges. Spoon about 2 heaped tsp of mincemeat into each pastry cup; no more than that, or it will bubble over the rim and weld the pies to the tray.

3. Re-roll the pastry (you may need to chill it for 10 minutes first, as it may have warmed up too much to roll) to the same thickness as before. Cut out Christmassy shapes – 7cm stars work well – making sure the shapes are in contact with the pastry cup, or they will float around as the pies bake. Lightly beat the remaining egg and brush on to the pies, then sprinkle with caster sugar.

4. Bake for 18–22 minutes until golden brown. Take out and leave to cool for a bit before releasing the pies from the tin.

PECAN PIE WITH SPICED RUM

You have to work hard to walk past one of these traditional American Thanksgiving pies. They are often made with bourbon and/or chocolate, but I reckon they taste pretty ace with a few splashes of spiced rum (but then, what doesn't?). We look forward to this every year.

SERVES 6–8

Ingredients

For the sweet pastry

1 quantity Sweet Shortcrust
    pastry dough (see page 128)
plain flour, to dust
1 large egg, lightly beaten

For the filling

100g golden syrup
100g maple syrup
100g golden caster sugar
50g soft light brown sugar
75g unsalted butter
3 large eggs
½ tsp vanilla bean paste
2 tbsp spiced rum
200g chopped pecans
100g pecan halves

Tool Kit

rolling pin
23cm loose-bottomed tart tin
baking beans (or about 300g of
    dried beans or raw rice)
pastry brush
wire cooling rack

1. Tip the sweet pastry dough on to a floured surface and gently knead for a minute or so, then shape into a flattish disc about 10cm wide. Wrap in cling film and leave in the fridge for 30 minutes to firm up.

2. Preheat the oven to 200°C/fan 180°C/gas 6.

3. Once the pastry has firmed up, take it out of the fridge. Roll it out on a floured work surface to a circle of roughly 30cm. Roll this up on to the rolling pin, then lay out into a 23cm loose-bottomed tart tin. Press the pastry into the tin, but leave the excess hanging over the edges. Leave in the freezer for 10 minutes, to allow it to firm up. Cut a disc of baking parchment larger than the tin, scrunch it up, then flatten it out again and lay into the tin. (Scrunching it up makes it more malleable when you add the baking beans.) Pour baking beans into the baking parchment and 'blind bake' in the oven for 15 minutes.

4. Take the tin out and remove the baking parchment and baking beans. Reduce the oven temperature to 160°C/fan 140°C/gas 3 and brush the base with beaten egg. Bake for 8 minutes, then take out and leave to cool. Increase the oven temperature to 200°C/fan 180°C/gas 6.

5. Meanwhile, make the filling. Measure the golden syrup and maple syrup into a saucepan. Add the sugars and butter and put over a low heat to melt. Allow to cool for 20 minutes, so it doesn't cook the eggs.

6. Beat the eggs, vanilla bean paste and rum together and stir into the cooled sugar mixture with the chopped pecans.

7. Pour the pecan mixture into the tart case and carefully arrange the pecan halves on the surface.

8. Bake for 35–45 minutes, until the pie has risen in the middle (this indicates that it has set). Keep an eye on the nuts, making sure they don't take on too much colour; if they are browning too quickly, cover with foil. Set on a wire rack until completely cool.

Extras

This pie really can take some mucking about with. The most important thing is cooking long enough for it to set. Once you've nailed that, you're sorted.

Even though it's called pecan pie, I sometimes replace the pecans with walnuts or macadamia nuts (the latter only if I'm feeling flush, mind).

Add 50g of cocoa powder to make chocolate pecan pie.

Replace the rum with coffee, orange or almond liqueur.

KEY LIME PIE

So delicious that my mouth is actually watering while I'm writing this. The brilliant zing you get from the lime filling will have you reaching for a second slice before you know what you're doing. Sadly there won't be one, because everyone else will have annihilated it and be demanding more. It tastes like summer.

SERVES 6–8

Ingredients

For the base

75g unsalted butter
175g ginger biscuits

For the filling

3 large egg yolks
400g condensed milk
finely grated zest and juice
    of 4 limes, plus more zest to
    serve (optional)

For the meringue
    topping

3 large egg whites
75g caster sugar

Tool Kit

food processor (optional)
23cm loose-bottomed tart tin
electric whisk
large piping bag (optional)
large star-tipped nozzle
    (optional)

1. Preheat the oven to 170°C/fan 150°C/gas 3½.

2. For the base, melt the butter in a saucepan.

3. Blitz the biscuits in a food processor (or put in a freezer bag and smash with a rolling pin) and mix into the butter well, then press into a 23cm loose-bottomed tart tin.

4. For the filling, beat the yolks in a bowl with an electric whisk until smooth and glossy. Beat in the condensed milk, lime zest and juice until smooth and well combined. Pour the mixture over the base.

5. Clean the mixer beaters thoroughly. Beat the egg whites and caster sugar together until stiff peaks form.

6. Gently load the meringue into a large piping bag fitted with a large star-tipped nozzle. Pipe it over the lime mixture. Alternatively, simply spoon the meringue over the filling, spreading and swirling to make peaks.

7. Bake for 15–20 minutes, or until the meringue begins to take colour.

8. Take out and cool completely before eating. If you have any limes left, grate some zest on to the top to serve.

Extras

This recipe uses egg whites and yolks in different layers; a simple and efficient use of ingredients and delicious, to boot! But you can miss out the meringue layer and bake the pie with just the lime filling. Top the cooled pie with 300ml of double cream whipped with 1 tsp vanilla extract and 50g icing sugar and serve with some finely grated lime zest. You can also replace the limes with two lemons, to make a lemon meringue pie. Have fun!

CHERRY AND PEACH PIE

I try to be sophisticated with puddings, but at the end of the day you just can't beat sweet fruit, pastry and custard. I came up with this recipe when I was trying to make a prettier-looking pie. The twisted top works so well with the dark cherry colour underneath. It's a bit fiddly, but worth it.

SERVES 6–8

Ingredients

For the crust

400g plain flour, plus
    more to dust
200g caster sugar
200g unsalted butter,
    chilled and chopped
1 large egg
1 tsp almond extract

For the filling

6 ripe peaches, or 400g can
    of sliced peaches in syrup
750g cherries
175g caster sugar, plus more
    to sprinkle
½ tsp ground cinnamon
1 tsp freshly grated nutmeg
4 tbsp cornflour

Tool Kit

rolling pin
24cm deep-sided round
    metal pie dish
pastry brush
wire cooling rack

1. Put the flour and sugar in a bowl. Rub in the butter with your fingers until the mixture looks like breadcrumbs. Crack in the egg, add the almond extract and use a knife to cut through the mixture, then turn the bowl and cut again, until it is dry enough to handle.

2. Tip out on to a floured work surface and knead for about a minute, then cut in half. Flatten each half out into a disc about 10cm wide, wrap in cling film and chill in the fridge for 30 minutes.

3. If you're using fresh peaches, peel, quarter and pit them. (If your peaches are really ripe, peel them as on page 82.) Halve and pit the cherries, then mix all the fruit in a large saucepan with the caster sugar and spices and 2 tbsp of water.

4. Set over a medium heat to cook for 10 minutes. Take 3 tbsp of the released juice and mix it with the cornflour in a cup. Pour back into the saucepan and cook for another 5 minutes. Leave to cool.

5. Preheat the oven to 180°C/fan 160°C/gas 4. Roll out one of the pastry discs on a lightly floured surface to 5cm wider than a 24cm deep-sided, round metal pie dish, moving it regularly so it doesn't stick. It should be about 3mm thick (the thickness of a pound coin). Roll the pastry on to the rolling pin, then lay on to the pie dish. Press it into the dish gently with your fingers so as not to break it (if you do break it, just press a little bit of excess pastry into the hole).

6. Pour the cherry-peach mixture into the pastry case, remembering to scrape out the gooey sugar at the bottom of the saucepan. The filling needs to be only the same level as the rim of the pastry, or juice will leak out during the bake. If you have too much, secretly eat it: cook's treat. Trim the excess pastry from the pie case.

7. Roll the second ball of pastry out on a floured surface and cut into strips about 15mm wide. Take each strip, twist it loosely, then coil around the surface of the pie, starting from the outside and working in. Dab the end of each strip with a bit of water and use your thumbs to pinch it on to the next as you spiral the pastry on to the pie. Cut out leaf shapes from the offcuts and lay these in the centre of the pie. Once the spiral of pastry has been laid, you will see quite a lot of filling through the top.

8. Bake for 35–40 minutes until the pastry has turned golden. Take out of the oven and set to cool on a wire rack, sprinkle with a little caster sugar and, when you can't take it any longer, carve it up and scoff it!

Extras
Cherry pie, is for my money, by far the best flavour you can get, especially with this almond-flavoured pastry thrown into the mix. You can make it with just cherries instead of the peaches (use 1kg of cherries). Knock up a bit of custard (see page 137) and you're good to go.

POURING CUSTARD

Of course this is not just for pies. Whatever you're having for pud will taste fantastic when you pour this all over it and it goes perfectly with my Cherry and Peach Pie (pictured opposite; see pages 134–5). Whatever you pour it over, this custard is super-easy and quick to make.

MAKES ENOUGH FOR 4
Ingredients
350ml whole milk
½ tsp vanilla bean paste
3 large egg yolks
1 tbsp caster sugar
2 tsp cornflour

Tool Kit
electric whisk

1. Add the milk and vanilla bean paste to a saucepan and set over a low heat.

2. Meanwhile, whisk together the egg yolks, caster sugar and cornflour in a heatproof bowl with an electric whisk. The egg yolks will whisk up to form a loose, light-coloured paste.

3. Once the milk is hot, but not quite boiling, pour into the heatproof bowl and whisk into the egg mixture.

4. Once fully combined, pour the custard back into the saucepan and heat over a medium heat, stirring constantly. The custard will thicken up to a pouring consistency.

5. Once thickened, pour into a jug and eat with pudding while it's still hot!

Extras
Flavour your custards! We do this at home all the time. Whether it's with a couple of tsp of cocoa powder beaten in after the custard has thickened up, or the infusion of lavender flowers, rose water or finely grated citrus zests into the milk (strained out before you pour it into the egg), custard can take plenty of flavour. Have fun with this simple recipe and make your puddings that little bit more brilliant.

8

TARTS

PINK GRAPEFRUIT CHEESECAKE

Cheesecakes are a really easy and delicious way of producing a cake without cooking (yes, I admit it, I've cheated here as this isn't actually *baked*). They are assembled, then chilled in the fridge, so if you're having a party they're a good way of having a cake to serve without using up a shelf in the oven. Citrussy cheesecakes such as this taste really light and are well worth having a crack at.

SERVES 8–10

Ingredients

60g unsalted butter, plus more
    for the tin
200g ginger biscuits
1 gelatine leaf
300g cream cheese
50g icing sugar
200ml double cream
finely grated zest and juice
    of 1 pink grapefruit
pomegranate seeds

Tool Kit

23cm loose-bottomed tart tin
rolling pin
electric whisk

1. Prepare a 23cm loose-bottomed tart tin by lightly buttering the base and sides, then sticking a circle of baking parchment to the buttered base.

2. Crush the biscuits in a freezer bag with a rolling pin and tip into a bowl. Melt the 60g of butter and pour into the crushed biscuits. Mix thoroughly with a spoon, then press into the prepared tin.

3. Cut up the gelatine leaf and soak in 30ml of hot water to soften.

4. Put the cream cheese and icing sugar in a bowl and beat with an electric whisk. Add the double cream and squeezed-out softened gelatine and whisk until the cream has thickened. Whisk in the grapefruit zest and juice, then pour into the tin.

5. Chill in the fridge for at least 2 hours.

6. Scatter some pomegranate seeds on top before serving.

Extras

This needs minimal decoration; it's simple and delicious. But if you can't bring yourself to leave well alone, you could add some pink food colour to the filling mix, or go for some good old-fashioned whipped cream to spoon plumply on top. Cheesecakes are so versatile. I always try and have ginger biscuits lying around the house to knock one up with whatever fruit I've got to hand.

TRAFFIC LIGHT JAM TARTS

These are so easy, always look bright and colourful, and taste delicious. This foolproof recipe will get the kids away from the TV for a bit on a Saturday, occupy them in the kitchen and not make too much mess. They are a good way to encourage beginners who are a bit nervy about this baking lark, without having to resort to cupcakes for the thousandth time. I've given three good, straightforward jam or curd recipes here, too, which are delicious and well worth making.

MAKES 12

Ingredients

For the strawberry jam
200g strawberries, hulled
200g jam sugar
2 tbsp lemon juice

For the lemon curd
60g unsalted butter
120g caster sugar
finely grated zest and juice of
    2 unwaxed lemons
1 tsp cornflour
2 large eggs, lightly beaten

For the lime curd
60g unsalted butter
120g caster sugar
finely grated zest and juice of
    5 limes
1 tsp cornflour
2 large eggs, lightly beaten
green food colour (optional)

For the tarts
200g plain flour, plus more
    to dust
85g unsalted butter, chilled
    and chopped
12 heaped tsp jam, curd or
    other sweet preserve

Tool Kit
hand whisk
8cm fluted cutter (optional)
12-hole muffin tin

1. To make the jam, put the strawberries, sugar and juice into a saucepan and place over a low heat. Stir to help the sugar dissolve, then bring to the boil and simmer for 5–10 minutes, testing to see if the jam is done by tipping a few drops on to a chilled saucer, waiting for 5 seconds, then pushing against the jam with your finger. If it wrinkles, the jam is done. If not, cook for a few minutes more, then test again. Take off the heat and allow to cool down.

2. To make either curd, put the butter, sugar, zest and juice into a saucepan and set over a low heat. Stir a little to help the sugar dissolve. Before all the butter has melted, take 1 tbsp of the citrusy mixture and mix up in a cup with the cornflour. Pour the beaten eggs and cornflour into the pan and gently whisk until the curd noticeably starts to thicken. (If making lime curd, you might want to add a little food colour now, for the 'traffic light' effect.)

3. As soon as the mixture thickens, pour into a bowl, cover and put in the fridge. Don't worry if it looks a bit thin; it will thicken as it cools.

4. For the tarts, put the flour into a large bowl and rub in the butter until the mixture resembles breadcrumbs. Mix in 2 tbsp of cold water, first using a spoon, then your hands to bring it together. Tip on to a lightly floured work surface and gently knead into a ball.

5. Roll the ball out to the thickness of a pound coin (about 3mm) and press out circles with an 8cm fluted cutter (or a 8cm-wide cup). The circles need to be bigger than the holes in a 12-hole muffin tin so you can push them into the shape of a tart. Roll out the offcuts to make enough cases to fill the tin, then pop it in the fridge for 10 minutes.

6. Preheat the oven to 190°C/fan 170°C/gas 5. Take the tart cases out of the fridge and spoon 1 heaped tsp of jam or curd into each (no more, or the jam will bubble over the sides and weld the tarts to the tin).

7. Bake for 15–20 minutes, or until lightly golden. Allow to cool. Remember, the jam is *hot*, so give them at least 30 minutes before you let little hands loose on them.

Extras
Once you've got the hang of the tart cases, you can experiment with lots more fillings: try crème pâtissière (see page 61) or even chocolate ganache (see page 64). You could also try making them in different shapes - flowers, hearts and so on - though you'll need novelty cutters for those.

CUSTARD TART

LEVEL 1

The wobble on a fresh custard tart might be one of the most inviting things you'll ever see on a plate. These are very simple to do and for my money can compete with many desserts that look much more sophisticated and are far harder to make. Once you've got one of these under your belt, a world of flavoured custards will open up to you. I've made this with an almond pastry, which adds a hint of interest underneath the creamy goodness of the custard and the mouth-watering nutmeg.

SERVES 8–10
Ingredients
For the almond pastry
200g plain flour, plus more
    to dust
100g caster sugar
50g ground almonds
100g unsalted butter, chilled
2 large eggs

For the custard
3 large eggs
120g caster sugar
350ml double cream
120ml whole milk
1 tsp vanilla bean paste
1 whole nutmeg

Tool Kit
rolling pin
23cm loose-bottomed tart tin
baking beans (or use about
    300g of dried beans or
    raw rice)
pastry brush
hand whisk

1. For the pastry, put the flour, sugar, almonds and butter in a bowl and rub in the butter until the mixture resembles breadcrumbs. Break in 1 egg and mix with a wooden spoon, then turn out on to a lightly floured work surface and knead for about a minute to combine.

2. Roll the pastry into a ball and flatten out to a disc about 15cm wide. Wrap in cling film and put in the fridge for 30 minutes to firm up.

3. Unwrap the pastry and roll it out on a floured surface to a circle about 28cm across. Roll gently, rotating the pastry regularly to stop it from sticking to the work surface. Roll the pastry up on to the rolling pin and lay in a 23cm loose-bottomed tart tin. Work the pastry into the edges of the tin, letting the excess hang over the edges. Prick the base with a fork to stop it bubbling up when cooking.

4. Put the tin in the fridge for 10 minutes to firm up. Preheat the oven to 200°C/fan 180°C/gas 6.

5. Line the pastry case with baking parchment and pour in a jar of baking beans to weigh down the base. Bake for 15 minutes.

6. Reduce the oven temperature to 180°C/fan 160°C/gas 4. Take the baking parchment and beans out of the pastry case and brush it with the remaining egg, lightly beaten, then bake for a further 8 minutes. Take out. Reduce the oven temperature to 150°C/fan 130°C/gas 2.

7. Make the custard: whisk together the eggs and sugar in a heatproof bowl. Place the cream, milk and vanilla bean paste in a saucepan and bring to the boil over a medium heat. Once boiling, remove from the heat and slowly pour the hot cream into the eggs, beating constantly. Skim the froth from the top and pour through a sieve into the pastry case. Grate nutmeg on to the surface; it only needs a light dusting.

8. Bake in the oven for 35–45 minutes or until the surface gives a slight wobble when shaken. Take out, let it cool, and eat!

Extras
Once you have got the hang of making the custard and getting it out of the oven before it turns to rubber, you're good to go. This classic tart takes some beating, but have a go at adding the finely grated zest of 2 unwaxed lemons to the milk and cream, heating as before, then letting it stand for 10 minutes before pouring through a sieve into the egg and sugar: it is delicious! You can make orange custard in the same way. I really like lavender custard, too, made by infusing 1 tbsp of lavender flowers in the milk.

BUILDER'S QUICHE

Not traditionally the manliest of foods, this is a firm favourite on site with me and the lads… but then again, free food is always welcome on a building site. Whenever we have a buffet at home, the quiche always gets hoovered up first. I can never seem to make enough of it.

SERVES 8

Ingredients

For the rich
**   shortcrust pastry**
240g plain flour, plus more
    to dust
½ tsp table salt
180g unsalted butter, chilled
    and chopped
2 large eggs, lightly beaten

For the filling
1 medium onion (about 150g),
    finely chopped
1 tbsp vegetable oil
sea salt and freshly ground
    black pepper
1 garlic clove, crushed
1 tbsp dried oregano
80g spinach
2 large eggs
150ml whole milk
150g Stilton cheese

Tool Kit
rolling pin
23cm loose-bottomed tart tin
baking beans (or use about
    300g of dried beans or
    raw rice)
wire cooling rack

1. Put the flour into a large bowl. Add the salt, then rub in the butter with your fingertips until the mixture resembles breadcrumbs. Add the eggs and mix well with a spoon until the pastry comes together. Turn out on to a lightly floured work surface and gently knead for about a minute. Flatten out into a disc about 16cm wide, wrap in cling film and put in the fridge for 30 minutes to firm up.

2. Unwrap the chilled pastry and roll it out on a floured surface into a 30cm circle. Roll the pastry up on to the rolling pin and lay into a 23cm loose-bottomed tart tin. Gently press the pastry in the tin, cut off the excess and prick the pastry base with a fork. Put in the fridge for 15 minutes to firm up. Preheat the oven to 200°C/fan 180°C/gas 6.

3. While the pastry is chilling, prepare the filling. Fry the onion in the oil over a medium heat until golden brown. Add salt and pepper to taste (remember the cheese is very salty, so be careful). Add the garlic and oregano, stir for a minute or two, then tip in the spinach; turning it over in the pan until just wilted. Set aside.

4. Beat the eggs and milk in a large jug. Cut the cheese into small chunks (less than 1cm). Add half to the jug, along with the spinach mixture. Set aside.

5. Lay a sheet of baking parchment in the tart tin and fill with baking beans. Bake for 15 minutes, then take out the baking beans and parchment and bake for a further 10 minutes.

6. Pour the quiche mixture into the cooked case and sprinkle the remaining half of the chopped Stilton on top.

7. Return to the oven for another 30 minutes until golden brown and risen (it will rise quite high, but don't worry; it comes back down when it cools). Take out and rest on a wire rack to cool. Don't try and eat this one hot; it needs some time to settle. It's great warm, or at room temperature.

Extras

Quiche is almost infinitely variable. Fill with different cheeses (Gruyère is a really good traditional one), shredded bacon, cooked chicken, or fish. Lay tomatoes, asparagus or olives on top. Chuck in loads of mushrooms, or 75g of chopped walnuts. The only things you need to keep unchanged are the pastry case and the amount of eggs and milk for the filling. Other than that, whatever you have in the fridge or the cupboard you can use, so have a go.

ASPARAGUS AND BACON TART

LEVEL 2

Open tarts made with puff pastry are very easy to do. I've devised this recipe with home-made puff, but if you're in a rush of an evening or pushed for time, make it with shop-bought all-butter puff pastry and it will taste just as delicious! When asparagus comes into season, please have a go at this for dinner one night; I promise you won't regret it.

SERVES 4–6
Ingredients
For the puff pastry
¾ quantity Puff Pastry
    dough (see page 115)
plain flour, to dust
1 large egg, lightly beaten

For the filling
1 small red onion,
    finely chopped
1 garlic clove, crushed
½ tsp sea salt
½ tsp freshly ground
    black pepper
25g basil leaves
100g cream cheese
9–10 asparagus spears, woody
    ends cut off
8 rashers of streaky bacon
a little olive oil

Tool Kit
rolling pin
tape measure (for the pastry;
    optional, but I find it
    really useful)
baking tray or sheet
wire cooling rack

1. Make the puff pastry as on page 115. While the pastry is firming up in the fridge for the final time, prepare the filling.

2. Put the red onion and garlic in a bowl with the salt and pepper. Coarsely chop the basil and mix into the bowl with the cream cheese until fully combined. Pop in the fridge.

3. Drop the asparagus spears into a saucepan of fiercely boiling water. Cook for a minute, then drain and drop into a bowl of cold water to cool right down. Leave them in water until it's time to lay them out.

4. Lightly fry the bacon in a dry frying pan. Try to keep the rashers straight, so it's easier to weave them through the asparagus later.

5. Preheat the oven to 220°C/fan 200°C/gas 7. On a lightly floured work surface, roll out the pastry to 30 x 25cm and lay on a baking tray or sheet lined with baking parchment. Bake for 10–12 minutes until golden brown and puffed up. Leave on a cooling rack until cold.

6. Return the pastry to the lined baking tray and spread out the cream cheese mixture with a spoon, leaving a clear 2cm border around the edges. It is fiddly at first, but once you've got some on, it gets easier.

7. Drain the asparagus and toss in a little olive oil, then lay the spears crossways in a neat row along the tart, with their spears pointing in alternate directions; try not to push the asparagus into the cream cheese yet. Now comes the fiddly bit. Weave the streaky bacon in between the asparagus spears; you'll need to lift a few spears up to get the bacon under them, but it is surprisingly easy once you get the hang of it.

8. Put back in the oven for 12–15 minutes until the asparagus is tender, then take out and eat while nice and hot. Yum!

Extras
This recipe looks fiddly, but I promise it is really easy and the woven topping looks great. If you don't have an extra few hours to muck about making puff, get a packet of the ready-made stuff. Puff tarts are a great way of knocking up a quick dinner. They taste far lighter than pizza, though that is a good place to look for flavour inspiration. Pretty much any pizza topping can go on this. Spread on pesto, or some cold chicken, add a few peppers…

Don't feel you're limited to savoury toppings: my mum makes a brilliant tart with pears and almonds and frangipane (see page 217): you're on to a winner! These get hoovered up in our house, and hopefully will in yours, too.

BANOFFEE TARTLETS

I often think banoffee gets a bit of a raw deal in the dessert world. I'm not sure why. Maybe it's the daft name; just not sophisticated enough to take seriously…? One thing is certain: it can taste delicious. I like baking these as individual tarts, then leaving them in the fridge and forgetting about them until dinner is ready. The way the cream, banana and caramel complement each other always cheers me up and anything that gives me the chance to make and eat a bucket-load of caramel is a winner.

MAKES 6
Ingredients
For the caramel filling
200g caster sugar
80g unsalted butter, chopped
120ml double cream

For the sweet
chocolate pastry
175g plain flour, plus more
    to dust
50g cocoa powder
¼ tsp table salt
100g unsalted butter, chilled
    and chopped
100g caster sugar
3 large eggs

To top
2 ripe bananas
250ml double cream
grated dark chocolate,
    to sprinkle

Tool Kit
rolling pin
set of 6 x 10cm loose-bottomed
    tartlet tins
baking beans (or use about
    300g of dried beans or
    raw rice)
pastry brush
wire cooling rack
electric whisk
small offset palette knife

1. Start by making the caramel. Put the sugar in a saucepan over a medium heat and melt it down. Try not to stir it but, as it begins to melt, swirl the saucepan around to keep it moving; this will avoid any parts getting burnt.

2. Once the sugar has melted and turned a light brown colour, reduce the heat to low and add the butter. This will boil and froth up, so mix with a spoon (it's OK to mix it now) until it settles down and is well combined. Still mixing, slowly add the cream until the mixture forms a rich brown caramel. It will still be quite liquid, but don't worry: it thickens as it cools. Set aside.

3. Now make the pastry. Mix the flour, cocoa powder and salt in a bowl. Rub in the butter with your fingertips until the mixture resembles breadcrumbs. Stir in the sugar, then break in 2 of the eggs. Mix with a wooden spoon until a rough dough forms.

4. Turn out on to a floured work surface and knead for 1–2 minutes until well mixed, but don't knead any further as you don't want to develop the gluten in the flour (that will toughen the pastry). Flatten the dough out into a disc about 15cm wide, wrap in cling film and put in the fridge for 45 minutes to firm up.

5. Remove it from the fridge and roll out on a floured surface to about 45 x 30cm. Cut it into 6 squares and lay them in 6 x 10cm loose-bottomed tartlet tins. Use your fingers to work the pastry well into the corners and let the excess flop over the sides. Prick the bottoms of the pastry cases with a fork and put in the fridge for 30 minutes to firm up.

6. Preheat the oven to 190°C/fan 170°C/gas 5 and cut out 6 circles of baking parchment, each about 15cm in diameter. Fold them across their centre point a few times (as if you were making a cut-out snow flake), then scrunch the paper up and open out flat again. Take the tartlet cases out of the fridge and place the circles of baking parchment in them. Fill these with baking beans, put them on a baking tray and 'blind bake' in the oven for 8 minutes. Beat the remaining egg. Take the tartlet cases out of the oven and remove the papers and baking beans. Brush them with a little beaten egg and return to the oven for another 8 minutes.

Continued…

7. Take out of the oven and cut the excess pastry from the edges of the tins with a serrated knife (be careful: the tins are hot!). Take the cases out of the tins and set on a wire rack to cool.

8. Once the cases are cool, divide the cooled caramel between them; filling to just below the top of the case (it doesn't matter if the caramel isn't cold; you just don't want it to be hot). Put in the fridge to cool and firm up the caramel.

9. Peel and slice the bananas (discs 5mm thick will do) and whip the cream in a bowl with an electric whisk until it forms soft peaks.

10. Once the caramel has cooled down enough to set, lay 6 discs of banana on each tart in a flower shape and spread the whipped cream on top with a small offset palette knife, sprinkling with grated chocolate to finish. Leave in the fridge until you want to serve them.

Extras

I really like the unashamed sweetness of these; they're simple and they don't muck about. I reckon that sweetening or flavouring the cream would be a step too far, but feel free to beat 25g icing sugar and ½ tsp vanilla extract into it if you have a super-sweet tooth.

One thing I do think adds an extra bit of fun is a smidgen of salt in the caramel. I love salty caramel! Make it in exactly the same way, but stir in ½ tsp of sea salt flakes: the flakes will stay whole, so every now and again you'll get a brilliant salty bite.

This caramel also keeps for at least two months in the fridge, so make some just to have around the house. You'll end up pouring it on everything (or just eating it off of a spoon in front of the fridge).

If I'm feeling particularly adventurous, I like to top these tartlets with a mass of spun sugar. A bit messy, but lots of fun! To make spun sugar, combine 125g caster sugar and 2 tbsp water in a saucepan. Don't stir it! Cook until it reaches 155°C on a confectionery thermometer, then remove from the heat. Using two forks, flick the sugar on to a sheet of baking parchment to make spun sugar, or twist around an oiled cylindrical metal utensil, or a ladle, to make sugar spirals or nests.

PATISSERIE FRUIT TART

Ever since I was a kid, I always wanted to make the sort of fruit tart you get in fancy French patisseries. I think they look spectacular! They are, in principle, pretty simple: sweet pastry tart case, set crème pâtissière and fruit. Precision is the key for this tart, not only in the cutting of the fruit to show it off at its most attractive, but also in a well-set filling and a thin but stable case. Make this to treat someone you love, or if you just feel like showing off.

SERVES 10

Ingredients

For the crème pâtissière
220ml whole milk
1 tsp vanilla bean paste
3 large egg yolks (save
    the whites)
50g caster sugar
1½ tbsp cornflour
150ml double cream

For the almond crust
150g plain flour, plus more
    to dust
75g unsalted butter, chilled
    and chopped
75g caster sugar
25g ground almonds
1 large egg, lightly beaten

For the fruit filling
4 kiwi fruits
200g (12 large) strawberries
100g blueberries
100g raspberries

Tool Kit
electric whisk
rolling pin
23cm loose-bottomed tart tin
baking beans (or use about
    300g of dried beans or
    raw rice)
pastry brush
wire cooling rack
piping bag

1. Start by making the crème pâtissière. Pour the milk into a saucepan, stir in the vanilla bean paste and set over a low heat. While the milk is heating (keep half an eye on it to make sure it doesn't boil) whisk the yolks with the sugar and cornflour in a heatproof bowl, using an electric whisk. They will turn slick and creamy.

2. Just before the milk is boiling, pour it into the egg mixture in the bowl, whisking constantly. Once the milk and eggs are fully mixed together, pour back into the saucepan and continue to heat over a low heat, mixing with a silicone spatula, until the custard thickens up.

3. Transfer to a clean bowl, lay cling film on the surface of the custard (to stop a skin forming) and put in the fridge to cool down.

4. Now for the almond crust. Put the flour into a large bowl and add the butter. Rub together with your fingertips until the mixture resembles breadcrumbs. Stir in the sugar and ground almonds, then the egg, until the mixture comes together as a soft pastry.

5. Turn the dough out on to a floured work surface and knead for about a minute to make sure it is fully mixed, then flatten into a 15cm disc, wrap in cling film and chill in the fridge for 30 minutes.

6. Peel the kiwis with a very sharp knife and slice them evenly and thinly. Hull the strawberries and slice them thinly lengthways.

7. Unwrap the pastry and roll out on a lightly floured surface, making sure to regularly rotate it as you're rolling (otherwise it will stick to the surface). Roll out to 28–30cm wide, then roll the pastry up on to the rolling pin. Lay the pastry in the tart case and gently work it into the tin with your fingers. Leave the excess hanging over the edge; it will stop the sides from wilting down the tin while cooking.

8. Pop the pastry case into the fridge for 15 minutes to firm up. Preheat the oven to 200°C/fan 180°C/gas 6.

9. Prick the pastry case with a fork, lay in a circle of baking parchment and fill with baking beans. Bake for 15 minutes.

10. Take the case out of the oven, reduce the oven temperature to 180°C/fan 160°C/gas 4 and remove the baking parchment and baking beans. Paint some of the egg white (saved from separating the eggs for the custard) on to the base and sides of the case and put back in the oven to bake for another 8 minutes.

Continued...

11. Take out of the oven, set on a wire rack and allow to cool down for 10 minutes before taking the pastry case out of the tin and allowing it to go cold.

12. Whip the double cream with an electric whisk until it forms soft peaks. Take the chilled custard out of the fridge, peel the cling film off and mix up with a silicone spatula. Fold in the whipped cream, a couple of tbsp at a time. Load into a piping bag and evenly pipe into the cold tart case.

13. Arrange the fruit on the crème pâtissière. This takes a little more planning than you'd think. It is very easy to just try and make a perfect circular pattern and leave it at that, but I reckon this looks a bit lazy and 1970s. I like to fan my sliced strawberries around the edges of the tart and then randomly place the rest of the fruit in. Start by arranging your larger pieces of fruit, then fill in gaps with progressively smaller fruits until all the crème pâtissière is covered. This will make the tart look much more interesting and appetising. Pop in the fridge to chill until ready to serve.

Extras

If you don't have access to loads of perfectly ripe fruit, don't despair! Halved strawberries laid all over a custard tart are magic just by themselves. I like to make seasonal versions with soft fruit from my garden: the tartness of a few redcurrants, blackberries and gooseberries really works with the smooth, sweet crème pâtissière.

Make individual tarts if you have small tartlet tins; these are a good challenge and always look as if you've made an effort (though the pastry for these will need a shorter time in the oven; keep your eye on them).

But, for my money, bigger is better. A good slice of this with a morning coffee is a pop of colour to cheer up even the most miserable rainy day.

9

SAVOURY PASTRIES

LAMB SAMOSAS

LEVEL 1

You can get samosas anywhere these days, which is ace, because when I was little they were more of a rare and exotic treat. There's nothing like fresh samosas, though, so have a go at making these. They really are delicious and are another excuse to muck about with filo pastry. This recipe is made with ready-made filo, as it is much thinner and far easier to use than filo you make yourself. This spiced lamb recipe is a good starter version that will hopefully show you how easy it is to fold samosas up and in what proportion to add the filling. Make these for a buffet and watch them get hoovered up.

MAKES 18
Ingredients

100g new potatoes
3 tbsp vegetable oil, plus
    2 litres more to deep-fry
1 onion, finely chopped
2cm root ginger,
    finely chopped
1 red chilli, finely chopped
1 tsp sea salt
200g minced lamb
1 tsp garam masala
½ tsp cumin seeds
2 garlic cloves, crushed
1 carrot, finely chopped
1 bunch of coriander,
    finely chopped
75g frozen peas
1 tbsp plain flour, plus more
    to dust
250g packet of ready-made
    filo pastry

Tool Kit

deep-fat fryer (optional)
cooking thermometer
    (optional)
wire cooling rack

1. Put the new potatoes in a small saucepan of boiling water and cook for 15 minutes, then drain and leave to cool.

2. Heat the 3 tbsp of vegetable oil in a pan over a medium heat and add the onion, ginger, chilli and salt. Fry for 5 minutes until the onion begins to soften. Add the lamb and fry for 5 minutes, turning, until browned. Add the garam masala, cumin, garlic and carrot, mix well and cook for 5 minutes. Dice the potatoes (smaller than 1cm). Stir into the pan with the coriander and peas, then cover and cook for 5 more minutes. Leave to cool with the lid on, so it doesn't dry out.

3. Set a deep-fat fryer to 170°C, or heat a large saucepan filled to a depth of 8cm with vegetable oil to 170°C on the hob. If you don't have a cooking thermometer, heat the oil until a small piece of white bread sizzles when dropped in. Keep a careful eye on the pan during frying. Mix the flour to a paste in a small bowl with 2–3 tbsp of water.

4. Gently unroll the filo on a lightly floured work surface. Use sharp scissors to cut a sheet into three strips lengthways (about 8cm wide), then cover with some cling film to stop it from drying out. Take each strip at a time and fold over one corner to make a triangle, then spoon in 1½ tbsp of filling (no more, or your samosas won't fold up) into the triangle 'pocket'.

5. Lay the filled filo on the work surface and fold up the triangle shape as neatly as possible. Before making the final fold, spread flour paste on to the open flap and fold it over to stick the samosa closed. Lay it down seam side up while you make the rest, or the flour paste will stick it to your work surface and you'll rip it when you pick it up.

6. Fry the samosas in batches of 3–4 at a time for 3–4 minutes, turning once, or until golden brown. Lay the samosas on a wire cooling rack lined with kitchen paper to soak up the oil while you cook the rest. Eat warm, or store in the fridge for a few days and reheat to serve.

Extras

I always make extra filling, to account for the inevitable scrumping that goes on while it cools. Don't feel obliged to make lamb; spiced vegetable samosas last longer in the fridge (replace the meat with the same weight of new potatoes). I urge you to get a cook's thermometer; they're dead cheap (just don't wash them with an abrasive cloth, or you'll scratch the numbers off).

CHEESE STRAWS

LEVEL 1

Another simple bake that you have to make loads of because they are so very easy to plough through. I prefer to make the pastry myself as you can incorporate cheese into more of the layers, which I think makes it puff better. Bake these to eat while you veg out in front of a movie on a Saturday night, or to be demolished at the start of any meal you care to serve. Once you can make them, though, I'm afraid you'll have the job because you'll keep being pestered for more.

MAKES 22

Ingredients

225g plain flour, plus more
   to dust
pinch of table salt
75g unsalted butter
75g lard
75g Cheddar cheese, grated
50g Parmesan cheese, grated
½ tsp cayenne pepper

Tool Kit

rolling pin
tape measure
2 baking sheets or trays

1. Put the flour and salt into a bowl and mix in 125ml of cold water thoroughly with a spoon until combined. Turn out on to a floured work surface and knead for 5 minutes until soft and elastic. Cover with cling film and leave to rest for 5 minutes.

2. Chop the butter and the lard into 1cm cubes and return them to the fridge; it's important they are cold.

3. Roll the dough out on to a floured surface to a 45 x 15cm rectangle. Try to get the edges as sharp and as straight as you can.

4. Remove the butter and lard from the fridge and place them evenly on the dough, covering two-thirds of the length of the pastry and also leaving a clear border around all the edges. Fold the plain dough over half of the buttered-and-larded section and press the edges to seal the butter in. Fold this layer over again to cover the remaining section and press down the edges all round to form a 15cm square of pastry. Turn by 90 degrees and roll out to 45 x 15cm again, then fold up into thirds as before, wrap in cling film and put in the fridge for 30 minutes to firm up.

5. Mix the cheeses with the cayenne pepper. Take the pastry out of the fridge and roll out on a floured surface to 45 x 15cm. Sprinkle the cheeses over two-thirds of the pastry, lengthways, and fold up as in the previous step. Return to the fridge for another 30 minutes.

6. Preheat the oven to 220°C/fan 200°C/gas 7 and line 2 baking sheets or trays with baking parchment. Take the pastry out of the fridge and roll out on a floured surface to 44 x 15cm. Cut into strips of 15 x 2cm. Twist each strip twice, place on the baking trays and bake for 15 minutes until golden and puffed up.

7. Eat as quick as you can, then make some more.

Extras

The good thing about these snacks is that you can flavour them however you want. I've spiced these up with cayenne, but you can also use English mustard powder or curry powder. Sprinkle them with poppy seeds or sesame seeds or any herbs you can find in the cupboard, for extra texture or taste. Be sure to twist them before cooking, or they will rise, topple over and all stick together. Have fun making these, but keep them away from the dog while they're cooling... My dog is usually good as gold around what I bake, but the moment these come out of the oven her nose starts twitching and I have to keep them out of reach.

PORK, FENNEL AND CHILLI SAUSAGE ROLLS

Honestly, what do you need to know about sausage rolls other than that they are flippin' delish? I used to only make them around Christmas, as that's when we had loads of spare sausagemeat in the kitchen. Now I make them all the time, mainly because they are quick, tasty and I can put in any flavour I like. Have a go, but make sure you share them, as scoffing the lot isn't the most slimming diet!

MAKES 16

Ingredients

**For the rich rough-
    puff pastry**

250g plain flour, plus more
    to dust

2 tsp lemon juice

100g salted butter, chilled

50g lard, chilled

1 large egg, lightly beaten

For the filling

300g sausagemeat

1 tsp fennel seeds, crushed

½ tsp chilli flakes

sea salt and freshly ground
    black pepper

Tool Kit

rolling pin

tape measure

pastry brush

wire cooling rack

1. Make the rough-puff pastry by mixing the flour, lemon juice and 125ml of water in a bowl with a spoon until combined. Tip out on to a lightly floured work surface and knead for a minute or so until smooth. Cover with cling film and leave to rest for 5 minutes.

2. Chop the butter and the lard into 1cm cubes and return them to the fridge; it's important they are cold.

3. Roll the dough out on a floured surface to a 45 x 15cm rectangle. Try to get the edges as sharp and as straight as you can. Remove the butter and lard from the fridge and scatter them evenly over the dough, covering two-thirds of the length of the pastry while leaving a clear border around all the edges. Fold the plain dough over half of the buttered-and-larded section and press the edges to seal the butter in. Fold this layer over again to cover the remaining section and press down the edges all round to form a 15cm square of pastry. Turn by 90 degrees and roll out to 45 x 15cm again, then fold up into thirds as before, wrap in cling film and put in the fridge for 30 minutes to firm up.

4. Once the dough has chilled, take it out of the fridge and do another 'turn, roll and fold' as described above, then return to the fridge for another 30 minutes.

5. Meanwhile, mix the sausagemeat in a bowl with the fennel seeds and chilli flakes, seasoning with salt and pepper. Tip out on to a well-floured surface and roll it in some flour to stop it being too sticky. Divide into 4 equal pieces and roll each piece in flour. Set aside.

6. After the pastry has had its second chilling, take out of the fridge and do one last 'turn, roll and fold'. Preheat the oven to 220°C/fan 200°C/gas 7. Roll the dough out on a well-floured surface to around 40 x 20cm and cut into 4 strips of 20 x 10cm.

7. Take each of the portions of sausagemeat and roll out to 20cm long with your hands. Put each of the long sausages on a piece of the pastry, then fold the pastry over the meat and seal the edges well with beaten egg; there should be enough pastry to get a 1–2cm overlap. Cut each into 4 sausage rolls each about 5cm long.

Continued on page 160...

8. Brush well with beaten egg and slash diagonally with a sharp knife to allow the rolls to expand as they cook. Bake for 25–30 minutes until golden brown.

9. Once cooked, place on a cooling rack quickly as they may be swimming in liberated sausagemeat fat, lard and butter (I never said they were healthy, just delicious). Squeeze a terrifying amount of brown sauce on a plate and get dipping.

Extras

Once you've got the hang of making rich rough-puff pastry, you're sorted with sausage rolls. These are flavoured with fennel seeds, mainly because I love that aniseedy taste, but feel free to flavour them with whatever you like, or leave out the chilli if you're not a fan of spicy food. Sage is a traditional choice and ground cloves work, too, as does apple. Some people add a dose of chutney or mustard. In fact, rhubarb chutney tastes brilliant in this combination. The main thing to do is to make loads. Friends will mysteriously turn up at the door once they find out you're baking these on a regular basis.

SAUSAGE, MUSHROOM AND TOMATO TEA-BREAK DANISH

In my line of work, we often start the day with a cup of coffee and a hastily grabbed Danish as we leg it through a petrol station and into the rush hour. Years of living like this has given me a broad knowledge of what the world of a quickly grabbed Danish has to offer. Petrol-station Danish do the trick; they fill a hole and keep us warm for a morning's work. Sweet ones are fantastic, don't get me wrong, but of a morning it just has to be savoury and – given the choice – it has to be these.

MAKES 8
Ingredients
For the Danish pastry dough
250g strong white bread flour, plus more to dust (optional)
250g plain flour
1 tbsp 'quick' yeast
2 tsp table salt
50g caster sugar
3 large eggs
120ml whole milk
250g unsalted butter, chilled

For the filling
8 chipolatas
100g button mushrooms, sliced
a little oil
Dijon mustard
200g tub of sun-dried tomatoes

Tool Kit
stand mixer fitted with dough hook (optional)
dough scraper (optional)
tape measure
rolling pin
pastry brush
2 baking trays or sheets
wire cooling rack

1. For the dough, mix the flours, yeast, salt and sugar in a bowl, making sure you add the yeast and salt to opposite sides of the bowl. Add 2 of the eggs, 60ml of cold water and the milk and mix with a wooden spoon. If you have a stand mixer, mix on medium speed with a dough hook for 8 minutes. If you don't, you can still make these but it takes a bit more work: mix on a floured work surface using a dough scraper to stretch out the dough, then your hands once it becomes less sticky, for 15–20 minutes until smooth and elastic. Wrap up the dough in cling film and put in the fridge for 1 hour.

2. Unwrap the dough and roll out on a floured surface to 60 x 20cm (a tape measure will be useful here).

3. Bash out the butter between 2 sheets of cling film, using a rolling pin, to 39 x 18cm. Regularly turn the butter and peel off and re-lay the cling film to stop it ripping (it's a right pain peeling ripped cling film off a thin layer of rapidly melting butter).

4. Lay the butter on the dough so it covers two-thirds of the surface lengthways and also leaves a clear border around all the edges, then fold the exposed one-third of dough over half of the butter, pressing the edges to seal the butter in. Fold the final one-third of butter-covered dough over to get 3 layers of dough, separated by 2 layers of butter, pressing down the edges all round.

5. Turn the dough by 90 degrees and roll out again to 60 x 20cm. Fold in thirds again, as before, to give 9 layers of dough. Wrap in cling film and return to the fridge for another hour.

6. Take out and roll out to 60 x 20cm on a floured surface again and fold in thirds again to get 27 layers, then turn through 90 degrees, roll out and fold to get 81 layers (!). Return to the fridge for at least 8 hours and up to 24 hours.

7. Fry the chipolatas and mushrooms in the oil, then leave to cool. Once cooled, cut each chipolata in half lengthways, then again widthways, to make 4 pieces per chipolata.

Continued...

8. Roll out the chilled dough to 60 x 30cm and cut into 8 squares of 15cm (you may need to rest the dough halfway through for 10 minutes allow you to roll it out far enough).

9. Spread a line of mustard diagonally down the middle of each square, then lay the chipolata pieces on top and cover with a few slices of mushrooms and sun-dried tomatoes.

10. Lightly beat the last egg and use it to stick the two opposite corners over the filling to form the Danish shape. Reserve any remaining egg. Place on 2 baking sheets or trays lined with baking parchment, leaving enough room between them for the pastries to grow. Cover each tray with a plastic bag – it should not touch the pastries but form a tent over them – and leave to rise at room temperature for 1½ hours, or until doubled in size.

11. Preheat the oven to 220°C/fan 200°C/gas 7. Liberally brush the pastries with beaten egg and bake for 15–20 minutes. Cool on a wire rack, then eat with brown sauce (not red, you philistines!).

Extras

The simple Danish shape described here works well if you're putting in large lumps of filling such as chunks of chipolata. You can also make pinwheels, by cutting diagonally in from each corner of your square of dough, not quite to the middle, then folding one point from each corner to the centre. You can make rolls from this dough, too, by rolling out to 60 x 20cm and spreading your desired filling out over the whole surface, then gently rolling up into one long sausage shape and cutting into 5cm-wide segments. Lay any of these shapes on to prepared baking trays and leave to rise as described in the recipe before baking.

If you're not a meat eater, don't despair; you can substitute the sausage for 200g of grated Cheddar cheese mixed with 50g of grated Parmesan cheese and it will taste delicious. Even if you are into meat, you can still sprinkle cheese on. No one's gonna stop you.

CHILLI CON CARNE PASTIES

LEVEL 3

These are proper Guy Fawkes Night fare, a real treat on a cold autumn evening. Invite some mates round for fireworks and pile these up for them to grab and scoff. Leave out some sour cream for people to dip them in, too. Pasties in one hand, sparklers in the other: sorted!

MAKES 12
Ingredients
For the rough-
puff pastry
150g salted butter, chilled and
    cut into 1cm cubes
150g lard, chilled and cut into
    1cm cubes
600g plain flour, plus more
    to dust
1 tsp salt
2 tsp lemon juice
1 large egg, lightly beaten

For the filling
500g minced beef
1 large onion, finely chopped
a little olive oil
1 red pepper, finely chopped
2 garlic cloves, crushed
1 chilli, finely chopped
400g can of chopped tomatoes
400g can of red kidney beans,
    drained and rinsed
½ tsp chilli flakes
2 tsp paprika
generous splash of
    Worcestershire sauce

Tool Kit
rolling pin
2 large baking sheets or trays
13cm saucer or bowl
pastry brush
2 wire cooling racks

1. For the rough-puff pastry, put the cubed butter and lard in a bowl and briefly mix. Put the flour and salt in a large mixing bowl and, using your fingertips, briefly rub in about one-quarter of the butter and lard (you should still see lumps of fat).

2. Add 300ml of cold water and the lemon juice and mix until it comes together to form a dough. Roughly shape the dough into a rectangle.

3. On a lightly floured work surface, roll out the dough into a rectangle about 3mm thick. Scatter the remaining lard and butter to evenly cover two-thirds of the length of the dough, leaving a clear border around all the edges. Fold the plain dough over half of the buttered-and-larded section and press the edges to seal the fat in. Fold this layer over again to cover the remaining section and press down the edges all round. Rotate the dough 90 degrees, then roll out into a rectangle as before and repeat the folding. Turn, roll and fold the dough twice more, then wrap in cling film and refrigerate for 30 minutes.

4. In a large pan, fry the minced beef and onion in the oil over a medium heat for about 5 minutes, or until the mince starts to brown. Add the pepper and fry for another 2 minutes, then the garlic and chilli for another 2 minutes. Add the tomatoes, beans, chilli flakes, paprika and Worcestershire sauce. Stir well, bring to the boil, then lower the heat and leave the sauce to reduce so the consistency isn't too wet. Allow to cool fully.

5. Take the cooled pastry from the fridge and repeat the rolling and folding one more time, then return it to the fridge for another 30 minutes.

6. Preheat the oven to 200°C/fan 180°C/gas 6 and line 2 large baking sheets or trays with baking parchment.

7. Roll out the pastry to about 3mm thick. Cut out 12 circles, about 13cm in diameter, using a small saucer or bowl as a guide (see opposite). Any off-cuts can be rolled out again to make more circles.

8. Brush the edges with beaten egg, then put about 3 tbsp of the cold chilli beef mix in the middle of each circle. You need enough to fill the pastry but not so much that it will split open. Fold the pastry over the filling to encase it, using the beaten egg to help the edges of the pastry stick. Crimp the seal with your fingers and place on a prepared tray. Repeat to make 12 pastries.

Continued...

9. Brush each pasty with more beaten egg and bake for about 40 minutes, or until golden brown. When cooked, transfer to wire racks to cool a little before serving.

Extras

Once you've got the hang of making this rough-puff and crimping it into pasties, the world is your oyster; you can pretty much fill them with anything. The most important thing to watch out for is that you don't make your filling too wet. I like to use chicken curry, but I've also used bolognese, minted lamb, or anything I've got left over in the fridge. It's a great recipe for using up the leftovers from a Sunday lunch. If you have the self-discipline (unfortunately I often don't), try making them with the leftovers from a Chinese takeaway crispy duck... pretty amazing. This recipe is for quite a large batch, but you can freeze half the filling and reduce the pastry quantities by half to make 6, if you prefer.

BEEF WELLINGTON

If you're feeling flush, you could do a lot worse than using a nice bit of fillet to make a Wellington. This is a massive treat of a dinner: succulent beef, wrapped in mushrooms and Parma ham, all encased in a big pillowcase of fluffy puff pastry. Just delicious! Make this if you're celebrating something special with friends. It's really not that difficult and the ingredients just sing on the plate. My little sister makes beef Wellington every Christmas Eve. I reckon she's got it down pat, so I've nicked a few aspects of hers for this recipe. Maybe this year we'll have a Wellington-off...

SERVES 4–6, DEPENDING HOW GENEROUS YOU'RE FEELING

Ingredients

For the filling

1kg good-quality beef fillet

2 tbsp olive oil

sea salt and freshly ground black pepper

2 tbsp vegetable oil

2 shallots, finely chopped

25g unsalted butter

225g button mushrooms

75ml white wine

1 tsp thyme leaves

150g Parma ham

For the pastry

1 quantity Puff Pastry (see page 115)

plain flour, to dust

1 large egg, lightly beaten

Tool Kit

food processor

small palette knife (optional)

tape measure (for the pastry; optional, but I find it really useful)

baking tray

rolling pin

pastry brush

1. Rub the beef with olive oil, then sprinkle with salt and pepper. Heat the oil in a large frying pan to just smoking, then put the beef in; it will spit, but keep the beef moving so it doesn't stick to the pan. Sear the beef on all sides until a rich brown colour forms: you really want to get some colour on here, so about 15 minutes spent in the frying pan is perfectly acceptable. Reduce the heat to low and set the beef aside to cool.

2. Put the shallots in the pan with the butter and ½ tsp more each of salt and pepper and cook until they are translucent.

3. Put the mushrooms in a food processor with the wine and blitz until smooth. Scrape into the frying pan. Cook for 5–10 minutes to expel some of the moisture, stirring the whole time. Once the mushrooms resemble a fine paste, stir in the thyme, take off the heat and set aside to cool.

4. Lay 2 large sheets of cling film on a work surface, overlapping each other by about 5cm, to make a large square. Lay out the Parma ham in a rectangle about 35 x 30cm, overlapping the slices. Using a small palette knife or a table knife, spread the reduced mushrooms over the ham, covering it totally.

5. Lay the beef in the middle of the mushroom/Parma ham rectangle and gently lift 2 corners of the cling film up to roll half the ham over the meat. Flatten the ham down with your hands and peel the cling film away to lie back down on the work surface.

6. Roll the other half of Parma ham over the beef in the same way. You should now have the beef totally wrapped in mushrooms and ham.

7. Fold the ends of the Parma ham neatly and roll up the cling film tightly so that it looks like a massive shiny sausage. Twist the ends of the cling film to seal the Wellington together and put in the fridge to cool while you make the puff. (If you're using packet puff, you still need to chill the beef for 1 hour.)

8. Make the puff pastry as on page 115.

9. Lay a sheet of baking parchment on a baking tray and take the wrapped beef and chilled puff pastry out of the fridge.

Continued on page 170...

10. Roll the pastry out to 35 x 30cm and peel the cling film off the beef. Gently lay the beef in the centre of the pastry. Put the beef on upside down: it should have a flattish surface that formed while it was in the fridge; this needs to be facing up.

11. Fold the pastry over the beef and stick together by liberally painting with beaten egg. Fold the loose ends over, too, and stick down with beaten egg.

12. Roll the Wellington over on to the baking tray, so the seams of pastry are now on the bottom and the top surface is smooth.

13. Paint the remaining beaten egg over the pastry, then slash the pastry quite deeply (but not all the way through) with a sharp knife. Put in the fridge to chill for 30 minutes. Preheat the oven to 200°C/fan 180°C/gas 6.

14. Take the Wellington from the fridge. Bake for 25 minutes until golden brown, then take out and allow to rest for 10 minutes before serving. This will give you a medium-rare Wellington, so if you like it cooked more or less, adjust the time to your taste.

15. Carve to serve and fight over who gets the last slice!

Extras

This is a winner. I absolutely love it. The mushroom paste (duxelles) is a really tasty complement to such a meaty dish and we always sneakily try and take more than our share of Parma ham. If you want, you can replace the duxelles with 200g of smooth chicken liver pâté, or 'meat butter' as one of our little cousins likes to call it! The most important thing to remember for this recipe is that you have got quite a dense lump of meat, so scaling up means you're going to need to increase the cooking time a lot. If you want to change up to a 1.5kg piece of beef, for example, the final bake time will be closer to 45 minutes. I've served this a few times for people who like their beef cooked medium, in which case I cut off their slices and just put them back in the oven for a bit longer.

10

SWEET PASTRIES

ROSE AND PISTACHIO BAKLAVA

I have a confession to make: I may be pathologically addicted to baklava. Living in north London, we are surrounded by enough different food traditions to make your head spin. I've had Turkish, Greek, Israeli and Moroccan versions of baklava within a few miles of my front door. This is my own 'north London baklava' recipe and it's simple. It uses shop-bought filo pastry for one reason only, and that is that every single person who ever gave me a hint or a tip or a nod about making baklava uses it, too.

MAKES ABOUT 36

Ingredients
200g granulated sugar
100ml water
2 tsp rose water
200g pistachios
75g icing sugar
1 tsp ground cardamom seeds
    (pop the seeds out of green
    cardamom pods and bash
    them small)
150g unsalted butter
250g pack of ready-made filo
    pastry sheets

Tool Kit
food processor
pastry brush
small baking tin (about
    25 x 16cm, preferably
    not non-stick)

1. First make the syrup. Dissolve the granulated sugar in the water in a saucepan over a medium heat. Add the rose water and simmer for 5 minutes, then take off the heat and leave to cool.

2. Put half the pistachios, the icing sugar and ground cardamom in a food processor and blitz for 30–60 seconds.

3. Melt the butter in a saucepan over a gentle heat, or in the microwave, and brush a layer on to a small, preferably non-stick baking tin (about 25 x 16cm).

4. Cut each filo sheet into 3 equal pieces to fit the shape of the baking tin and lay the first in the bottom. Brush with butter. Repeat until 4 layers of filo have been laid down. Sprinkle over half the blitzed pistachio mix.

5. Butter and lay 6 more sheets of filo into the tray, then spread the remaining pistachio mix on top. Sprinkle over the remaining 100g of whole pistachios and spread them out evenly. Layer and butter the rest of the filo on top (there should be about 6 more sheets).

6. Preheat the oven to 200°C/fan 180°C/gas 6. Take a very sharp knife and cut halfway through the baklava in horizontal lines around 3cm apart. Cut diagonal lines (again halfway through) across this to make diamond-shaped baklava. Bake for 40 minutes until light brown.

7. Leave to cool for 30 minutes in the tin before pouring all the syrup evenly over the top. Allow to cool completely. The longer it is left, the more syrup will soak in, and the more delicious it will be.

8. Take the sharp knife and cut over the indentations you left earlier, this time going all the way through to the bottom. Serve the diamond shapes on a plate.

Extras
Another favourite baklava flavouring is toasted almonds and walnuts with orange blossom water: it's off the hook! Honey and lemon work brilliantly together, too. This diamond shape is by far the simplest to make, though many others exist. I really like rolled baklava, which are fun to figure out how to do. If you're going to attempt a rolled baklava, layer your filling on top of about 4 sheets, then roll, instead of just rolling up one long sheet; this will stop the baklava from tightening up and allow it to grow as it cooks.

BASIC CHOUX PASTRY

The first few goes I had at choux pastry were disastrous: it wouldn't rise, or it would rise and then fall, or it would just burn. Luckily for you, I've managed to iron out those baking errors over the years to leave this simple method. Apparently it is a bit unconventional, but it's always worked for me. Perfect for éclairs, profiteroles or anything else you fancy filling with cream or dipping in chocolate.

**MAKES 12 ECLAIRS OR
36 PROFITEROLES**

Ingredients

75g unsalted butter, chopped
    into pieces
¼ tsp table salt
100g strong white bread flour
3 large eggs

Tool Kit

stand mixer fitted with paddle
    attachment
piping bag fitted with a large
    (ideally 15mm
    round) nozzle
wire cooling rack

1. Pour 175ml of water into a saucepan over a medium heat and add the butter and salt. Sift the flour on to a square of baking parchment, big enough to pick up by its opposite corners with no flour falling out.

2. Once the saucepan has started to boil and the butter has melted, pour the flour in, reduce the heat to low and vigorously mix over the heat for 2–3 minutes to form a thick paste. Tip it into a heatproof bowl, lay cling film on the surface and leave to cool to room temperature. Tip it into the bowl of a stand mixer fitted with a paddle attachment. Turn the mixer to medium speed; the paste should crumble.

3. Once it has crumbled to smallish (about 5mm) lumps, turn the mixer to full speed and crack in the first egg. Allow it to fully combine before adding the second. While it is being beaten in, crack the third egg into a bowl and beat thoroughly with a fork. When the second egg has been fully combined, gradually add the third egg a few tbsp at a time. The mixture will begin to form a smooth, pipeable paste.

4. Once you have tipped about half of the third egg in, turn the mixer off and scoop out some choux with a spatula. Give it a shake, and see if it is loose enough to slip off, leaving a 'V' shape (see left). You may need more egg, or you may not, so keep checking for that telltale 'V'. Once it is the correct consistency, scoop into a piping bag fitted with a large (ideally 15mm round) nozzle and chill. It keeps for a few days.

5. When ready to bake, preheat the oven to 220°C/fan 200°C/gas 7. If you're making éclairs, mark out their lengths on baking parchment, spacing them out well, as they will inflate loads in the oven. (If you're making profiteroles, pipe 'blobs' rather than 'sausages'.)

6. Pipe even lines – or blobs – of choux on to the parchment, either using a sharp knife to chop the ends off each éclair, or quickly pulling the piping bag up at the ends. Using a wet finger, smooth down any points that stick up, so they don't burn in the oven.

7. Bake for 15 minutes. Reduce the oven temperature to 200°C/fan 180°C/gas 6, open the door to let the steam escape, then close it and bake for another 20 minutes.

8. Once baked, set on a wire rack. Cut the éclairs in half as soon as they are cool enough, or use a skewer to poke a hole in the bottom of each (this goes for profiteroles, too). This allows steam to escape, rather than soaking into the pastry and making it collapse.

9. Once cool, fill and dip them in whatever your heart desires...

IRISH CREAM PROFITEROLES

LEVEL 1

Profiteroles are a great go-to dessert if you're hosting, as they can be made in advance and stuck in the fridge (plus they last for 5 days, unfilled, in an airtight container). Serve these at the end of an evening of good food and talking rubbish and you'll not go wrong. *(Pictured overleaf.)*

MAKES AROUND 36
Ingredients
275ml whole milk
75ml Baileys Irish Cream
    liqueur
4 large egg yolks
75g caster sugar
2½ tbsp cornflour
1 quantity Basic Choux Pastry
    (see page 176)
200ml double cream
100g dark chocolate (70 per
    cent cocoa solids)

Tool Kit
stand mixer fitted with paddle
    attachment (for the choux)
large piping bags
2 baking sheets or trays
electric whisk
long-nosed nozzle

1. Start by making the custard filling. Pour the milk into a saucepan with the Baileys and set over a medium heat. Bring to a simmer, then take off the heat and leave to infuse for 10 minutes.

2. Meanwhile, put the egg yolks, caster sugar and cornflour in a heatproof bowl and whisk them together.

3. Once the milk has infused, pour it into the egg mixture, whisking constantly, then pour it back into the saucepan and set over a low heat. Stir constantly, using a silicone spatula, until the custard thickens, then quickly scrape into a clean bowl, lay cling film on the surface to stop a skin forming, and put in the fridge to cool.

4. Scoop the choux pastry into a large piping bag and cut a 1cm hole in the end of the bag. Pipe and bake 36 profiteroles as on page 176.

5. Once cooked, set on a wire rack. Use a skewer to poke a hole in the bottom of each, about 5mm across, to allow steam to escape.

6. Whip the double cream with an electric whisk until it achieves soft peaks. Take the cooled Baileys custard out of the fridge and fold in the whipped cream, a couple of tbsp at a time. Load into a piping bag fitted with a long-nosed nozzle and pipe into each profiterole.

7. To make the chocolate topping, roughly chop half the chocolate and put in a heatproof bowl over a pan half-full of water (do not let the bowl touch the water). Set over a medium heat and melt the chocolate. Meanwhile, finely chop the remaining chocolate. Once the chocolate in the bowl has melted, immediately take off the heat. Dry the bottom of the bowl and stir in half the finely chopped chocolate. This should take about 1 minute to melt in. If it melts in faster than that, let the chocolate stand for 5 minutes to cool off before adding the remaining chopped chocolate. This will temper the chocolate.

8. Dip the top of each profiterole in chocolate and allow it to set before serving to your very happy friends.

Extras
Baileys custard should be part of your repertoire if for no other reason than because it's delicious and easy. If you fancy other flavours, you can infuse custards with orange (see overleaf) or star anise (see page 189). Whatever you fill profiteroles with, I can heartily recommend dipping them in chocolate, as above, or caramel (see page 38), or salted caramel. If you're feeling fun, roll them in popping candy or crushed nuts after they've been dipped. Just make sure you've stashed a few in the kitchen for when everybody has gone home.

ORANGE, WHITE CHOCOLATE AND CARDAMOM ÉCLAIRS

I was really glad to get some white chocolate and cardamom ganache into this book, not only because it goes really well with the orange custard, but also because my wife and I can generally be found huddled around a bowl of it with a spoon and a guilty look on our faces...

MAKES 12

Ingredients

For the choux

1 quantity Basic Choux Pastry
(see page 176)

For the orange crème pâtissière

250ml whole milk

finely grated zest of
2 large oranges

3 large egg yolks

50g caster sugar

2 tbsp cornflour

150ml double cream

For the ganache

150g white chocolate

150ml double cream

6 cardamom pods

Tool Kit

stand mixer fitted with paddle
attachment (for the choux)

large piping bags

15mm round nozzle

electric whisk

2 baking sheets or trays

wire cooling rack

large star-tipped nozzle

1. Place the choux pastry in a large piping bag fitted with a 15mm round nozzle and leave in the fridge.

2. Now make the custard. Put the milk in a saucepan with the orange zest and set over a low heat, stirring occasionally. Once almost simmering, take off the heat and leave to infuse for 10 minutes.

3. Meanwhile, put the egg yolks in a heatproof bowl with the caster sugar and cornflour and whisk using an electric whisk (this is awkward to start with, but it turns smooth after a while). After 10 minutes has passed, pour the infused milk through a sieve into the heatproof bowl with the egg mixture, whisking all the time. Pour the custard into a clean saucepan over a low heat, stirring with a silicone spatula until it thickens. Pour into a clean bowl, lay cling film on the surface (to stop a skin forming) and leave to cool in the fridge.

4. Preheat the oven to 220°C/fan 200°C/gas 7. Cut baking parchment to fit 2 baking sheets of trays and, on each sheet, mark out 6 lines, 12cm long and 4cm apart. Flip the parchment over, so the lines are underneath. Pipe éclairs, using the lines as a guide. Bake as on page 176. As soon as they are cool enough, cut each in half using a long serrated knife. Lay on a cooling rack to dry out.

5. Make the ganache by breaking the white chocolate into pieces and putting it in a heatproof bowl. Pour the cream into a saucepan and set over a medium heat. Meanwhile, take the seeds out of the cardamom pods and crush them either with a mortar and pestle, or put them between 2 sheets of cling film and crush with a rolling pin. Once the cream has started to boil, pour it over the white chocolate, add the cardamom and mix until the chocolate melts and the mixture becomes smooth. Pop in the fridge to cool (it will thicken up).

6. Take the custard out of the fridge and mix with a spatula. In a separate bowl, whisk the cream until it forms firm peaks, then fold this into the custard a couple of spoonfuls at a time. Load it into a piping bag fitted with a large star-tipped nozzle. Pipe the orange custard on to the bottom layer of each éclair, then press on the tops.

7. Mix up the ganache with a spoon and load into another piping bag. Snip the end to give a 1cm opening and pipe a broad line over each éclair. Keep them hidden in the fridge until you're ready to watch family and friends descend into a *Lord of the Flies*-like madness as they fight for the last one!

CROISSANTS

OK, these take a little time and require forward thinking, but make them at home and you'll be ruined for supermarket versions forever. I like to make mine on a Friday evening when I get in from work. You can knock up the dough, go out for the night while they chill, then bake them for breakfast over the weekend: perfect! If you've got friends staying, bake a few batches, show off in the morning, then relax. You've done the hosting bit and can order takeaways for the rest of the weekend…

MAKES ABOUT 18
Ingredients
1 quantity Danish Pastry
      Dough (see page 161)
plain flour, to dust
1 large egg

Tool Kit

stand mixer fitted with dough
      hook (for the dough;
      optional)
dough scraper (for the dough;
      optional)
tape measure (for the dough)
rolling pin
2–3 baking sheets or trays
pastry brush
wire cooling rack

1. Make the Danish pastry dough as on page 161. Chill the dough in the fridge for at least 8 hours and up to 24, although overnight is probably best.

2. Line 2–3 baking sheets or trays with baking parchment, then take the pastry out of the fridge and roll out on a well-floured work surface to 60 x 30cm. Allow to rest for 5 minutes, then cut lengthways to make 2 strips of 60 x 15cm.

3. On each strip, cut triangles out crossways that are 12cm wide at the base. You should get 18 triangles in total with 4 off-cuts (see diagram opposite).

4. Make each croissant by gently stretching each triangle lengthways and rolling it up from the broad end first. Lay out on a prepared baking sheet or tray with the thin end of pastry tucked underneath. Lay each pastry on the trays, allowing room for them to at least double in size; if you don't have enough trays, you can lay a batch on some baking parchment, or you can bake the croissants in 2 batches.

5. Cover each tray with a plastic bag – it should not touch the dough but should form a tent around it – and leave to rise for 1½–2 hours until well risen and springy when poked with your finger.

6. Preheat the oven to 220°C/fan 200°C/gas 7 and beat the egg. Lightly brush each pastry with egg and bake for 16–18 minutes until golden brown and puffed up. Cool on a wire rack.

Extras
Once you've got the hang of croissants, they can become a bit of a compulsion… don't be surprised if you find yourself up at five in the morning on a week day cutting up a batch for breakfast. The classic croissant shape is easy to master, as long as you remember to stretch out your triangle of dough before you roll it up. My favourite version of this recipe is almond croissants. It is a simple extra to add, but sadly will have you up at 5am again (sorry). All you need to do is knock up a half-quantity of Frangipane (see page 217) and you're good to go. When you're stretching out your triangles of dough, spread 1 tbsp of this on top, then roll up as usual. Before it goes in the oven, sprinkle flaked almonds on top of the egg wash, so they stick. If you're planning on buying friends or allies at work, use these as a secret weapon: they never fail!

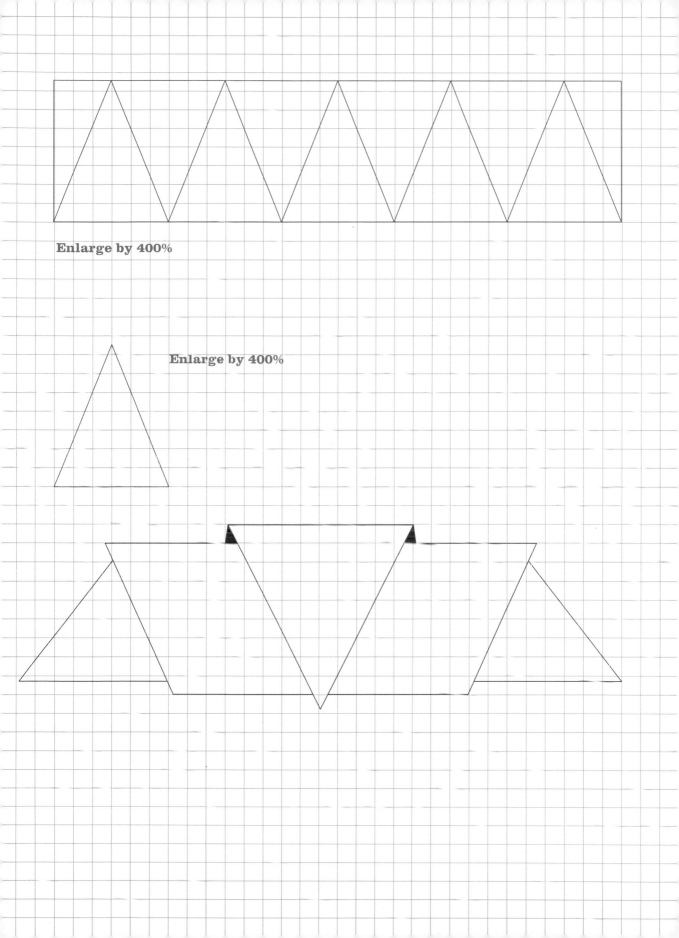

Enlarge by 400%

Enlarge by 400%

PLUM DANISH

When I was a teenager, I had a job in a bakery as a washer upper. I'd get in at 4.30am and go to a hot, noisy kitchen full of people who had already been up for hours and start washing up after them. Plum Danish always remind me of those days and the fun I used to have as a goofy but hopefully hard-working employee of the man who first showed me that baking could be brilliant. Cheers, David Anstee, wherever you are!

MAKES 8

Ingredients

1 quantity Danish pastry
 dough (see page 161)
4 ripe plums, halved and
 stones removed
plain flour, to dust
200g marzipan (for home-
 made, see page 61)
1 egg, lightly beaten
100g apricot jam
100g icing sugar
1 tbsp lemon juice

Tool Kit

stand mixer fitted with dough
 hook (for the dough;
 optional)
dough scraper (for the dough;
 optional)
tape measure (for the dough)
rolling pin
2 baking sheets or trays
wire cooling rack
piping bag

1. Make the Danish pastry dough as on page 161. Chill the dough in the fridge for at least 8 hours (or up to 24 hours).

2. Cut each plum into eighths, lengthways.

3. Roll out the chilled dough on a floured work surface to 60 x 30cm and cut it into 8 squares of 15cm (you may need to rest the dough halfway through for 10 minutes to allow you to roll it out far enough).

4. Roll out the marzipan to a 16cm square and cut it into 8 strips. To assemble the Danish, lay a marzipan strip diagonally on a dough square and add 4 plum pieces.

5. Using a little dab of water, stick the 2 opposite corners over the filling to form the Danish shape. Place on 2 baking sheets or trays lined with baking parchment, leaving enough room between them for the pastries to rise.

6. Cover each tray with a plastic bag – it should not touch the pastries but form a tent over them – and leave to rise for 1½ hours, until doubled in size.

7. Preheat the oven to 220°C/fan 200°C/gas 7. Liberally brush the Danish pastries with beaten egg and bake for 15–20 minutes.

8. Meanwhile, put the jam into a saucepan with 1 tbsp of water and heat up over a low heat.

9. When the pastries are cooked, take out of the oven and set on a cooling rack. Paint the hot jam on to the pastries.

10. While these are cooling, make the icing by beating the icing sugar and the lemon juice together. Once smooth, transfer to a piping bag and pipe on to the cooled pastries.

Extras

This recipe should set you in good stead for experimenting. The simple folded shape is a classic, and gives you room to stuff it with anything you fancy. As well as plums, I like to make these with a simple custard (see page 205) and some peach halves. Apples and pears also go well, as do raspberries and blueberries. Or fill them with sultanas, nuts and honey spiced with nutmeg and cinnamon. Or use slices of rhubarb with slivers of ginger in syrup, for which you can also use some of the ginger syrup to make the icing, instead of lemon juice.

APPLE STRUDEL

This has been a favourite of mine since I was a teenager. My mate Ross used to be borderline addicted to them and his mum went through a stage of having one cooked and chilled in the fridge for him when he got home from school. As a ravenous teenager, I'd make sure I walked home from school with him. We'd cut a strudel in half and eat it cold while standing in front of the open fridge and getting crumbs all over the floor. Nowadays we're much more refined and, sometimes, the strudel even makes it to the table on a plate. This is an old recipe that I've always liked, with the added fun of making the pastry and weaving the strudel closed. If you don't fancy the extra work, buy some ready-made pastry.

SERVES 6
Ingredients
For the pastry
⅔ quantity Puff Pastry
    dough (see page 115)
plain flour, to dust
1 large egg, lightly beaten

For the filling
1 large cooking apple
1 tbsp lemon juice
75g sultanas
50g flaked almonds
100g light brown muscovado
    sugar
1 tsp ground cinnamon
1 tsp freshly grated nutmeg
1 tsp caster sugar, to sprinkle

Tool Kit
rolling pin
tape measure (optional, but
    I find it really useful)
ruler
baking tray
pastry brush

1. Follow the instructions on page 115, rolling out your puff pastry dough to about 45 x 15cm each time.

2. To make the filling, peel, core and chop the apple into cubes of roughly 1.5cm. Put in a bowl and stir in the lemon juice. Add the sultanas and the flaked almonds and stir together.

3. Sprinkle in the brown sugar, cinnamon and nutmeg and stir thoroughly. The juice from the apples will mix with the brown sugar, making a sauce. Preheat the oven to 200°C/fan 180°C/gas 6.

4. Roll out the pastry on a floured work surface to a 30cm square. Using a ruler and a sharp knife, make horizontal cuts about 1.5cm apart down either edge of the pastry about 8cm into each side.

5. Lay the apple mixture down the middle of the pastry (on the uncut portion), neatly piled so that it isn't covering the cuts and is about 1cm away from the top and bottom edges.

6. Fold each strip of pastry diagonally over the apple mixture, weaving the 2 sides together until all the pastry is covered (see right).

7. Fold the last 2 ends underneath the strudel and lay it on a baking tray lined with baking parchment (don't put it on an unlined tray, or you'll be chipping it clean for weeks!). Brush with the beaten egg, then sprinkle with the caster sugar.

8. Bake for 35–40 minutes until golden brown. Eat hot, or allow to cool and put in the fridge for hungry teenagers.

Extras
These spiced strudels can be another good way of using up any dried fruit you've got languishing in the cupboard. I think they work really well with dried apricots, too. One of my other favourite strudels is a summer fruit version, with 100g blackberries, 100g raspberries and 100g blackcurrants. For that one I wouldn't recommend the weaving method, as the filling is so wet that it will never hold it in. Instead, roll it up in the uncut rectangle of pastry, fold the edges underneath (stuck together with egg) and slash the top to allow steam to escape. Once you get the hang of strudels, you'll be able to fire them out pretty rapidly, which you'll soon be asked to do once people find out how good they taste.

PAINS AU CHOCOLAT

I don't think I've ever said, 'Fancy a pain au chocolat?' and heard anything other than a resounding 'Yes!' in reply. I'm sure there are people who prefer something a bit less flaky, delicious and chocolatey at breakfast, but somehow I've managed to either avoid them, or just unconsciously cut them out of my life. Just to make these extra special, I've added passion fruit, which goes so well with chocolate.

MAKES 15
Ingredients
For the dough
1 quantity Danish Pastry
     Dough (see page 161)
plain flour, to dust
1 egg, lightly beaten

For the ganache
100g dark chocolate (70
     per cent cocoa solids)
100g double cream
3 ripe passion fruit

Tool Kit

stand mixer fitted with dough
     hook (for the dough;
     optional)
dough scraper (for the dough;
     optional)
large piping bag
tape measure (for the dough)
rolling pin
2 baking sheets or trays
wire cooling rack

1. Make the dough (see page 161). Put the dough in the fridge to chill for at least 8 hours, although overnight is probably best.

2. Make the passion fruit ganache by breaking the chocolate up into pieces and putting into a heatproof bowl. Heat the cream in a saucepan until boiling, then pour on to the chocolate and gently stir until a smooth, glossy ganache has formed.

3. Cut each passion fruit in half and scoop the pips and flesh into a sieve. Using the back of a spoon, work the passion fruit juice through the sieve and discard the pips. Gently fold the juice into the ganache (don't work this too much, or it will split) and load into a piping bag.

4. Take the chilled pastry out of the fridge and roll out on a well-floured work surface into a rectangle of 50 x 30cm. Allow to rest for 5 minutes, then cut into 15 squares of 10cm.

5. Pipe 2 lines of ganache on to each square of pastry (see right).

6. Roll each square up into a sausage. Try to separate the 2 lines of ganache with the edge of your pastry (the first bit you roll), as traditional pains au chocolat have 2 cores of chocolate.

7. Lay the pastries on to 2 baking sheets or trays lined with baking parchment, giving them loads of room to rise (they can double or triple in size) and cover with a plastic bag; this shouldn't touch the pastries, but form a tent around them.

8. Leave to rise in a cool place (not the fridge, but possibly the coldest, gloomiest room in the house) for about 2 hours.

9. Preheat the oven to 220°C/fan 200°C/gas 7, liberally brush each risen pastry with beaten egg and bake for 16–20 minutes or until plump, risen and brown.

10. Take out of the oven, set to cool on a wire rack, then eat with a cuppa and some grateful mates.

Continued...

Pains au Chocolat continued...

Extras

If you want to pare down this recipe, you can drop the passion fruit and cream and just sprinkle 200g of chopped chocolate on to the dough before you roll it up. One thing I like to do is to cook down 3-4 peeled, cored and chopped sweet pears in a saucepan until they become sticky and jam-like, allow to cool, then pipe it on the dough, sprinkle chocolate on top, and roll up as described. The sweet pear really works with dark chocolate.

FIG AND ANISE MILLEFEUILLE

I always thought millefeuille was just too fiddly to bother with. I was wrong! It is actually quite straightforward to make. As long as you know a couple of the knacks, these individual millefeuilles will turn out very nicely indeed. They are often a good opportunity to muck about with flavours and see which combinations work. This recipe is the result of one of my own experiments and I reckon it's a good'un. Remember, precision is the key for these, so keep your hands steady and get your tiny spirit levels out, because today you're mainly building pastries!

MAKES 10
Ingredients
For the pastry
⅔ quantity Puff Pastry dough
   (see page 115)
plain flour, to dust
1 large egg, lightly beaten
icing sugar, to dust

For the custard
170ml whole milk
3 star anise
2 egg yolks
35g caster sugar
1½ tbsp cornflour
100ml double cream

For the figs in syrup
4 baby figs
finely grated zest and juice of
   1 orange
50g light brown muscovado
   sugar
1 cinnamon stick

Tool Kit
rolling pin
tape measure (optional, but
   I find it really useful)
hand or electric whisk
2 baking trays
wire cooling rack
piping bags

1. Follow the instructions on page 115 to make the pastry, rolling it out to about 45 x 15cm each time and chilling in the fridge.

2. Now for the custard. Pour the milk into a saucepan with the star anise and set over a medium heat. Bring to a simmer, then take off the heat and leave to infuse for 10 minutes. Put the egg yolks in a heatproof bowl and whisk with the caster sugar and cornflour, using a hand or electric whisk.

3. Once the milk has infused, fish out the star anise and pour the milk into the egg mixture, whisking as you do so. Pour back into the saucepan and set over a low heat. Stir constantly, using a silicone spatula, until the custard thickens up, then quickly scrape into a clean bowl. Lay cling film on the surface of the custard (to stop a skin forming) and put in the fridge to cool.

4. While the pastry is chilling in the fridge, you can poach the figs. Cut each fig into sixths, put in a saucepan with the orange zest and juice, sugar and cinnamon stick and set over a low heat. Once simmering, cook for 8–10 minutes, occasionally turning the figs. Fish the figs out of the saucepan and lay on a plate. Put in the fridge to cool.

5. Preheat the oven to 220°C/fan 200°C/gas 7. Line a baking tray with baking parchment and take the pastry out of the fridge. Roll it out on a floured surface to a neat rectangle 30 x 25cm and lay this on the baking tray. Lay another sheet of baking parchment on top of this and weigh it down with another baking tray to stop the pastry from puffing up too far. Bake in the oven for 10 minutes.

6. Take the tray off the top of the pastry and return to the oven for another 10–12 minutes until golden brown and cooked through. Remove from the oven and take the pastry off the tray and off the baking parchment. Set on a wire rack to cool down.

7. Returning to the custard, whip the cream with an electric whisk until it forms soft peaks. Take the now-cooled custard out of the fridge and fold in the whipped cream, a couple of tablespoons at a time. Load into a piping bag and snip the end to make an opening about 5mm in diameter.

Continued...

8. Once the pastry is completely cooled, put it on a chopping board and carefully cut into 3 rectangles of 25 x 10cm. Cut each of these into 10 pieces, each 10 x 2.5cm, to give 30 neat fingers of puff pastry. Some of the outside ones may be a bit ragged, but those are generally the baker's treats!

9. Assemble each pastry: pipe 14 small blobs (two rows of 7) of custard on to the bottom layer of pastry. Lay the next layer on top and pipe on another 14 blobs of custard.

10. Take the figs out of the fridge and cut each segment in half (giving you 48 segments). Lay segments of fig on top of the custard, all facing in the same direction (see right). You might have a few fig pieces left over, depending on size.

11. Lay a third layer of pastry on top and dust with a little icing sugar. Repeat to assemble all the pastries.

Extras

I'm not going to lie; I'm very taken with anise custard. I hope you will be, too. Infusing custards is something I'm becoming a little obsessive about these days and this recipe is a doozy. There are no rules: if you can strain it out of custard, you can use it to flavour that custard, so go mad. You can of course use ready-made extracts instead of infusions, but be careful of adding too much extra liquid as it can split a custard, which is always a shame.

And you don't have to use custard. You can always whip up some cream and sweeten and flavour that instead, if you prefer.

I am a big fan of figs in loads of things and I think they go really well in this recipe. Poach them in whatever sounds interesting. I quite like adding a couple of tbsp of Pernod to the mix for this one; just be careful not to overdo it or it can blast out the flavour of the figs.

Finally, and I know this goes without saying, but don't feel compelled to make your own puff unless you really want to. Ready-made all-butter puff pastry from a packet works well for these and will knock off a lot of time if you're making them for a party. The most important thing is that you actually have a go at making them. They are delicious, delicate and look ace, so get to it!

11

PUDDINGS

FRENCH MERINGUE

Meringue is one of those magic ingredients that always takes me back to my childhood. Whether it was the soft top of a lemon meringue pie, a fruity pavlova or an Eton mess (usually the result of a failed pavlova in our house), this simple mixture of egg whites and sugar was always something to look forward to. Now I am older, and frankly braver/more irresponsible in the kitchen, Italian meringue is one of my favourite things to make. The smooth, rich, marshmallowy delight means the empty bowl is licked until it gleams! The added bonus of Italian meringue is that, if you want to take it a step further, you can beat in butter and flavours to make Italian buttercream meringue… possibly the best three words in the language. In this small section, we'll make French and Italian meringues. They will be enough to open up pretty much any meringue-based fun you're looking to have.

MAKES 6 REGULAR MERINGUES OR ABOUT 2 PAVLOVA BASES

Ingredients

3 large egg whites
100g caster sugar

Tool Kit

electric whisk (optional)
2 baking trays
large piping bag and nozzle (optional)
palette knife (optional)

1. Start by preheating the oven to 120°C/fan 100°C/gas ½. Yes, really that low, as you are going to dry the meringue out rather than cook it. Next beat the egg whites with an electric whisk (or a hand whisk if you're super-fit) until they form soft peaks.

2. Gradually add the sugar, about 1 tbsp at a time, continuing to beat until the meringue becomes glossy and thick. The meringue is ready when you can confidently tip the bowl over your head, safe in the knowledge that you won't get a face full of sugary egg white.

3. Line a baking tray with baking parchment (not greaseproof paper, or the meringues will stick). Depending on what you're intending to make, either load the meringue into a large piping bag or use a palette knife to smooth the meringue out into your desired shape. Now, one friend of mine pipes hers using a large star-shaped nozzle and different food colours to make hundreds of coloured meringue kisses out of each batch. These are awesome, and good for decorating cakes or putting in party bags.

4. Bake in the oven for ages – easily 1½ hours, and up to 2 hours for large, thick meringues. Once done, take out and allow to cool.

5. Release from the baking parchment by peeling the parchment off the meringues, rather than pulling the meringues off the parchment. Meringue is brittle and paper isn't, so be careful not to crack the meringues at this stage.

ITALIAN MERINGUE

LEVEL 1

Great fun to make, and not as hard as it seems. There are a couple of pitfalls that you might come across every now and again, but there are also loads of ways to recover meringue if you muck it up, so don't worry! This recipe makes quite a lot, but I find that if you make it in smaller quantities there is more room for error. For this recipe, you will need a confectionery thermometer. Now I know that can be a pretty intimidating piece of kit for some people. In fact, I used to be proper scared of it when I was just starting out, but they are easy to use, and you should definitely get one.

MAKES 6 REGULAR
MERINGUES OR ABOUT
2 PAVLOVA BASES

Ingredients

180g caster sugar

3 large egg whites

1 tsp cream of tartar, or 1 tbsp
    lemon juice

Tool Kit

confectionery thermometer

stand mixer fitted with
    whisk attachment

piping bag and nozzle
    (optional)

1. Start by putting 150g of the sugar and 60ml of water into a small saucepan with a confectionery thermometer (the smaller the saucepan the better, so the bottom of the thermometer can be submerged). Set over a medium-high heat and allow to heat up. The temperature will rise quite quickly until the sugar reaches 100°C when the water boils, then more slowly until the sugar reaches 121°C. (This may be indicated as 'soft ball' on your thermometer.)

2. Meanwhile, whisk the egg whites and remaining 30g sugar in the bowl of a stand mixer fitted with the whisk attachment. Once they begin to form soft peaks, add the cream of tartar or lemon juice (these are both acidic, helping the meringue maintain its structure).

3. Once the egg whites have formed stiff peaks and the sugar has reached 121°C, it's time to cook the eggs! Turn the mixer on to full power and pour a steady stream of the molten sugar into the bowl. Make sure you don't hit the whisk with the sugar, as this will shoot the sugar all around the sides of the bowl, welding it there so it doesn't cook the eggs.

4. Once all the molten sugar has been added, the bowl should be pretty hot. Leave the mixer on full speed until the bowl has cooled fully; this should take around 10 minutes.

5. Once cooled down, you can either spoon the meringue into a piping bag for use (it is now totally safe to eat as you have cooked the eggs), or you can go crazy and add some flavour and butter for Italian buttercream meringue (see below).

Extras

If you want to turn Italian meringue into Italian meringue buttercream (and if you do, it'll change your life), take 250g (yes 250g!) of unsalted butter at room temperature and whisk it into the Italian meringue on high speed, about 25g at a time, until fully combined. The buttercream can be flavoured with 45ml of a liqueur of your choice, or strong coffee, or 1 tsp of flavourings or extracts. Be careful with rose or lavender essences, though, as they can make the meringue taste soapy. Best use only ½ tsp of those.

Once you've flavoured it, load it into a piping bag and keep it out of the fridge until using, or the butter will firm up and you won't be able to pipe it. It will last for a few hours in the bag, or a few days once piped and refrigerated.

ORANGE BLOSSOM CREME BRULEE

Back when I was younger and fitter – and, frankly, irresponsible – I accidentally signed up for the Paris Marathon one evening after we'd had a few drinks. Luckily, I wasn't alone; my wife and two of our friends were also full of wine and bravado and, since none of us wanted to back down, there we were. The marathon went as well as can be expected, considering it was France, where they give you small cups of hot wine around the 38km stage (seriously? wine?). We all survived, felt suitably chuffed with ourselves and spent the next day creaking around Paris looking for somewhere to sit down. This is when we found a little bistro on the Île Saint-Louis where we had a classic lunch of onion soup, beef bourguignon and then these lovely orange blossom crèmes brûlées. The crème brûlée was fantastic and here it is… well, as close as I can get to it after seven years of trying.

MAKES 6

Ingredients

500ml double cream
finely grated zest of 1 orange
5 large egg yolks
70g caster sugar, plus more
    for the tops
2 tsp orange blossom water

Tool Kit

large roasting tin
6 ramekins
electric whisk
cook's blow torch (optional)

1. Preheat the oven to 160°C/fan 140°C/gas 3. Place 6 ramekins in a large roasting tin and set aside.

2. Pour the cream into a heatproof bowl, add the orange zest and heat over a saucepan half-filled with water. Stir occasionally.

3. In a large jug, beat together the egg yolks and the 70g of caster sugar with an electric whisk until the mixture turns light and glossy.

4. Once the cream gets close to boiling, pour through a sieve into the egg mixture, whisking constantly. Stir in the orange blossom water, then divide the custard between the ramekins. Pour hot (not boiling) water into the roasting tin, so it comes about halfway up the sides of the ramekins; be careful not to get any water in the custard.

5. Carefully put the roasting tin containing the ramekins in the oven and bake for 45–55 minutes until the custard has set, but still retains a wobble in the middle. Take out of the oven and leave to cool for 1 hour, still in the roasting tin, then take them out and put in the fridge for at least 2 hours to cool.

6. Before serving, sprinkle 2 tsp of caster sugar evenly on to the surface of each crème brûlée and either pop under a hot grill until the sugar caramelises or blast with a blow torch. The melted sugar will be very hot, so don't go digging into it the moment it has browned or, if you do, don't come moaning to me.

Extras

This is always good to do at a dinner party, because the hard work is finished early, leaving the showy bit (blow-torching) when you've got your mates round. It is important to bake these in a tin of water or you'll end up with orange-flavoured scrambled eggs. Orange blossom water can be found in supermarkets, but don't overdo it, or it will be overpowering. If you don't fancy flavouring and – let's face it – custard is pretty good as it is, add 1 tsp of vanilla bean paste instead of the orange zest and flower water. Or you can infuse 1 tbsp lavender in the cream, but remember to strain it out or you'll be picking lavender flowers out of your teeth all night. You can also plop a few raspberries or blackcurrants in each ramekin before pouring in the custard, to give a few fruity bursts.

STICKY TOFFEE PUDDING

When I was a kid, our school used to serve sticky toffee pudding every now and then at lunchtime. It was always a treat and had us bolting it down as fast as we could, so we could sneak up and try to score seconds. I still have the same attitude to this sweet, dense, sticky pud and at home all decorum goes out of the window as we fight for who gets an extra share. 'Combat eating' becomes really intense when my wider family eats together: once you have me, my sisters and all the little cousins around a table, it is a dog-eat-dog situation when this pud appears. A nostalgic sticky treat.

SERVES 6–8

Ingredients

For the pudding

225g pitted dates

200ml of boiling water

1 tsp bicarbonate of soda

1 tsp instant coffee

75g unsalted butter, softened, plus more for the dish

140g dark brown muscovado sugar

1 tsp vanilla bean paste

2 large eggs

175g plain flour

1½ tsp baking powder

1 tsp ground cinnamon

1 tbsp cocoa powder

For the butterscotch sauce

50g unsalted butter

100g dark soft brown sugar

100ml double cream

2 tsp lemon juice

Tool Kit

ovenproof dish, about 1½ litre capacity (mine is 27 x 23cm)

electric whisk

food processor

1. Roughly chop the dates and put them in a bowl with the boiling water, the bicarbonate of soda and coffee. Stir well and set aside for 20 minutes to soak.

2. Preheat the oven to 180°C/fan 160°C/gas 4. Liberally butter an ovenproof dish of about 1½ litres in volume (mine is 27 x 23cm) or line a similar-sized baking tin with baking parchment.

3. Beat together the butter and brown sugar in a large bowl with an electric whisk until lighter-coloured and fluffy. Add the vanilla bean paste and thoroughly beat in the eggs, one at a time.

4. Sift together the flour, baking powder, cinnamon and cocoa powder and fold them into the batter with a silione spatula.

5. Pour the dates – along with their soaking liquid – into a food processor and blitz down to a smooth purée. Fold into the batter, then carefully scrape into the prepared dish or tin.

6. Bake for 35–40 minutes, or until a cocktail stick comes out clean when poked into the centre.

7. While the pudding is cooking, make the butterscotch sauce. Melt the butter in a saucepan over a low heat. Once it has melted, add the brown sugar and cream, then increase the heat to medium and continue to stir until the mixture begins to boil. Whisk the mixture over the heat for 2–3 minutes using the electric whisk, then add the lemon juice and whisk for another 2–3 minutes. Pour the sauce into a heatproof jug and serve with the pudding.

Extras

This rich, dark and delicious pudding is ideal for a cold winter's evening or a long weekend's slobbing out in front of the TV. The dates gives this pud its unmistakable stickiness and make it a real winner. If you can get them, use fresh Medjool dates for extra stickiness, but the regular type work brilliantly, too. If you fancy your puddings a bit more dirty and mouth-watering, then add 1 tsp of salt to the butterscotch sauce for a little more of a grown-up flavour. If you can't find, or just don't like, dates, you can replace them with plump sultanas or sticky prunes and it will still taste lovely. Hopefully this will become a family favourite for you just as much as it is for us; just try to maintain a little decorum at the table while you're piling into it...

BLACKBERRY, ELDERFLOWER AND MINT PAVLOVAS

So, it's late summer. You're having a barbecue and serving salads, leaving the oven free for ages. Why not make these for pudding? This light dessert is so delicious, you won't believe your mouth. They are very easy to make, but look great. You can also make them a day in advance and keep them in the fridge. The combination of elderflower, blackberry and mint is so refreshing that, even though these contain about a metric ton of whipped cream, you'll leave the table feeling light and happy.

MAKES 6
Ingredients
For the meringues
3 large egg whites
100g caster sugar
purple gel food colour
75g icing sugar
250ml double cream
100g blackberries

For the syrup
100g caster sugar
25g mint leaves
3 tbsp St Germain elderflower liqueur (or elderflower cordial)

Tool Kit
baking tray
electric whisk
large piping bags
large star-shaped nozzle
wire cooling rack

1. Preheat the oven to 120°C/fan 100°C/gas ¼ and line a baking tray with baking parchment (not greaseproof; the meringue will stick to that).

2. Whisk the egg whites in a bowl using an electric whisk until stiff peaks form. Still whisking, add the caster sugar, a couple of tbsp at a time. Take some gel colour (about ¼ tsp) and fold into the mixture to give a pale violet; be careful with the gel – it is very potent.

3. Sift in the icing sugar and gently fold it in just until smooth. Do not continue to mix it, as you don't want to knock out too much air. Load into a large piping bag fitted with a large star-shaped nozzle.

4. Pipe 6 nests on to the baking tray, each 10–12cm in diameter, starting in the centre of each nest and spiralling out to form the base. Then pipe a rim of meringue around the edge of each.

5. Put the meringues into the oven for 1 hour 45 minutes to dry out. Drying out is the key to a good French meringue (see page 194).

6. Meanwhile, make the syrup. Put the sugar in a pan with 75ml of water over a medium heat. Coarsely chop 20g of the mint leaves (keep back 6 sprig tips for decoration) and add to the syrup with the elderflower liqueur. Simmer for 10 minutes, then take off the hob and leave to cool. Strain the syrup through a sieve to remove the leaves.

7. Once the meringues have cooked, take them out of the oven, gently peel off the baking parchment and set on a wire rack to fully cool. It is much easier to peel the paper away from the meringues than vice versa: the paper bends, whereas the meringues crack!

8. Once all the elements of the pavlova have cooled, whip the cream until it reaches soft peaks. Fold 3 tbsp of syrup into the cream and load into a large piping bag. Pipe cream into the nests, then sit 5 blackberries in the centre of each. Drizzle 1 tbsp of syrup over the blackberries and poke the saved tips of mint into the cream.

Extras
I made these for my family recently and I have never seen a pudding get so efficiently annihilated in my life, hence it being a bit of a shoo-in for this book. I can recommend them for a party, as you can make all of it in advance. I really like cocktail pavlovas. Make mojito pavlovas, or, if you can make a tequila sunrise pavlova that works, give me a shout. We'll be friends for life!

CHOCOLATE OOZING PUDDINGS

These are a guilty pleasure in our house. If we've got mates coming round, I usually knock up a batch and we pile into them once the kids have gone to bed (sorry, kids, if you're reading this in the future). The trick is to bake them for just the right amount of time to get a really good flow of chocolate coming out when you cut into them. They are not particularly sophisticated, but I bet you anything you couldn't resist one if it was put in front of you.

MAKES 6

Ingredients

For the raspberry coulis

200g raspberries

2 tsp lemon juice

2 tbsp caster sugar

For the puddings

200g unsalted butter, plus
    more for the moulds

cocoa powder, to dust

300g dark chocolate (70 per
    cent cocoa solids)

4 large eggs, plus 4 large
    egg yolks

110g caster sugar

75g plain flour

200ml double cream

icing sugar, to dust

Tool Kit

6 mini pudding moulds

electric whisk

large piping bag and nozzle

baking tray

1. Make the coulis by heating the raspberries, lemon juice, sugar and 3 tbsp of water in a saucepan until boiling. Reduce the heat and simmer for 5 minutes. Strain through a sieve into a bowl, pushing the berries through with a spoon and leaving the seeds behind.

2. For the chocolate fondants, butter 6 mini pudding moulds and lightly dust with cocoa powder.

3. Break up the dark chocolate and chop the 200g of butter and put them in a heatproof bowl over a saucepan of water on a medium heat (the bowl must not touch the water). Stir until they melt.

4. In another bowl, whisk the eggs, egg yolks and caster sugar with an electric whisk until smooth, light-coloured and creamy. Fold in the chocolate mixture using a spatula, then sift the flour and fold it in.

5. Load the fondant mixture into a large piping bag and pipe a layer of fondant on to the base of each pudding mould, then 3cm up the inside edges. Spoon 3 tsp of raspberry coulis into the middle of the mould, then pipe the rest of the fondant mixture into the mould up to 1cm from the top. Refrigerate for 30 minutes.

6. Preheat the oven to 190°C/fan 170°C/gas 5. Place the puddings on a baking tray and bake for 13 minutes. Make sure you set an oven timer!

7. Meanwhile, whip the cream with the electric whisk until soft peaks have formed.

8. Take the fondants out and carefully release from the moulds: lay a plate on top of a mould and turn them both over, then gently twist the mould off the pudding. Dust each fondant with a little icing sugar (this is especially useful for camouflage if you haven't buttered the pudding moulds enough and the fondants come out a bit rough).

9. Serve each fondant with a neat dollop of whipped cream.

Extras

One of the main constraints in modifying these puddings is the requirement to have oozing middles. If you bake them for too long, you get a dense chocolate sponge; bake them for too short a time and they end up raw and disintegrate when you turn them out. The timing may take practice, but 13 minutes is perfect in my oven. These work really well when filled with a fruit coulis. Sharp raspberries, blackcurrants and blackberries cut through the rich chocolate. Or try straining the juice out of 4 passion fruits and stirring it into the batter to give a citrus zing. If you are a pure chocoholic, just omit the fruit!

POSH BREAD AND BUTTER PUD

LEVEL 3

So, you've gone mad baking bread and have loads left over? Time for some bread and butter pudding! At home we stick it in the oven as soon as dinner comes out, so we can threaten the kids with no pud until they've finished their greens. (You don't necessarily have to threaten your kids, but it does add spice to dinner!) And yes, you're right, it's not a level 3 pud... unless you make your own brioche or panettone to go in it, that is. But don't feel obliged; you can buy it in (in which case, it's a level 2!).

SERVES 6–8
Ingredients
75g sultanas
finely grated zest of 1 orange
4 tsp orange liqueur (such as Grand Marnier; optional if you're sharing it with kids)
50g unsalted butter
6 slices of brioche or panettone (ideally home-made, see pages 32 and 41)
350ml whole milk
50ml double cream
1 tsp vanilla bean paste
3 large eggs
50g caster sugar
1 tsp freshly grated nutmeg

Tool Kit
ovenproof dish, about 1½ litre capacity (mine is 27 x 23cm)
electric whisk
large roasting tin

1. Mix the sultanas and orange zest in a bowl with the orange liqueur and set aside to soak.

2. Preheat the oven to 200°C/fan 180°C/gas 6 and use half of the butter to liberally butter an ovenproof 1½ litre dish (mine is 27 x 23cm). Spread the rest of the butter on both sides of each slice of brioche or panettone.

3. Lay the slices of brioche or panettone in the prepared dish, sprinkling the soaked sultanas between each slice. Scrape out any zest and liquid left in the bowl and spread them over the bread.

4. Pour the milk and cream into a saucepan and add the vanilla bean paste. Set over a medium heat and heat until just-not-quite boiling. While the milk is heating up, beat the eggs and sugar together with an electric whisk. While still gently whisking, pour the warm milk and cream into the beaten egg mixture. Once the mixture is combined, gently and evenly pour it over the bread and leave to soak for 10 minutes.

5. Grate the nutmeg over the soaked bread and put the dish in a large roasting tin.

6. Pour hot (but not boiling) water into the roasting tin, so it comes about halfway up the side of the dish; be careful not to get any water in the custard.

7. Bake for 35 minutes, then take out, slice and eat while hot.

Extras
Bread and butter pudding is one of those recipes that always seem to happen spontaneously of an evening. Mainly because the essential ingredients are usually knocking around in the kitchen – bread, milk, butter and eggs – so as long as you can come up with some inspiration to flavour them, you're good to go. It works with any bread, but I prefer to make it with bread made from enriched dough such as brioche. I really like adding orange flavours to bread and butter puddings, but you can also try a fairly big slug of Baileys instead (about 50ml) and it will taste ace. Or flavour with marmalade and 1 tsp of whisky if you're feeling a bit grown-up. Once again, as with a lot of recipes in this book, feel free to root around in the cupboard and whack in dried and candied fruits or chocolate chips. Sprinkle sugar mixed with cinnamon, nutmeg or ginger on top, but just make sure you have a go. There's no excuse not to, so make it, enjoy it, and save some for the kids.

RHUBARB AND CUSTARD ENTREMETS

STAR BAKE

Entremets are a bit bonkers, to be honest. They are a labour of love, and a good way of showing off as many skills as you can in as small a bake as possible. If I've got a spare Saturday and really feel like getting stuck in in the kitchen, I'll make a batch of these. So far, no two batches have been the same, mainly because there are so many choices and combinations to be made that it almost feels like a wasted opportunity to recreate a version that has already worked. Hopefully, this recipe will act as a jumping-off point for you to start mucking about with your own entremets. These flavours are pretty classic, but the construction can be a bit fiddly, so precision is the watchword. Have fun with this recipe, and remember, you can always look back through the book and incorporate different skills and flavours into your own insane versions.

MAKES 6

Ingredients

For the custard
90ml whole milk
½ tsp vanilla bean paste
1 large egg yolk
20g caster sugar
2 tsp cornflour
75ml double cream

For the sponge
a few drops of flavourless oil
2 large eggs
½ tsp vanilla bean paste
50g caster sugar, plus more
    to sprinkle
50g plain flour
½ tsp baking powder
pink gel food colour
yellow gel food colour

For the biscuit base
65g unsalted butter, softened
2 tbsp caster sugar
100g plain flour, plus more
    to dust
1 tsp ground ginger
30g ground almonds

For the rhubarb filling
100g rhubarb

Continued...

1. Start by making the custard. Put the milk and vanilla bean paste in a saucepan over a low heat. In a heatproof bowl, whisk together the egg yolk, sugar and cornflour with an electric whisk until creamy and combined. Once the milk is near simmering, pour it into the bowl with the egg mixture, whisking constantly, then pour back into the pan and mix with a silicone spatula over a low heat until thickened. Quickly scrape it into a clean bowl and lay cling film on to the surface of the custard to stop a skin forming. Put in the fridge to cool.

2. Now start the sponge. Line a Swiss roll tin with baking parchment; I put a few drops of oil on the tray to stick the parchment down. Whisk the eggs, vanilla bean paste and sugar in a bowl using the electric whisk until very pale and with a lot of volume (this will take 5 minutes of constant whisking). Sift together the flour and baking powder and gently fold into the whisked egg mixture with a spatula; make sure you pick up all the flour from the bottom of the bowl, but try not to over-work the batter or you will knock out the air.

3. Take 3 tbsp of the mixture and put in a bowl. Mix some pink gel food colour into this (I use about the tip-of-a-knife's worth) and load into a piping bag fitted with a 2mm nozzle. Pipe thin lines of pink sponge mix on to the lined Swiss roll tin and put in the freezer for 30 minutes. Mix yellow gel food colour (around ¼ tsp) into the remaining sponge batter.

4. While the sponge is freezing, make the biscuit base. Preheat the oven to 180°C/fan 160°C/gas 4. Put the butter and sugar in a bowl and beat with a wooden spoon until creamy and combined. Sift together the flour and ginger and mix into the butter with the ground almonds, beating with a wooden spoon until the mixture comes together. Once it has come together, stop mixing: you don't want to develop the gluten in the flour or your biscuit will be tough.

5. Roll out the biscuit mixture on a floured work surface to a rectangle about 25 x 15cm and 5mm thick. Line a baking tray with baking parchment. Gently lift the biscuit dough on to the tray and bake it for 12 minutes; it will just be taking colour by this time.

20g unsalted butter

20g caster sugar

1 tsp cornflour

**For the ginger
    cream layer**

125g mascarpone

125ml double cream

30g icing sugar

1 tsp ground ginger

For the jelly layer

100g rhubarb

30g caster sugar

1 gelatine leaf

pink gel food colour (optional)

**For the finishing touches
    (optional)**

100g white chocolate

Tool Kit

Swiss roll tin (check it fits in
    your freezer)

electric whisk

2 piping bags

2mm icing nozzle

baking trays

6 x 6cm-diameter
    entremet or cooking
    presentation rings

2 wire cooling racks

ruler

long-nosed nozzle

small offset palette knife

patterned chocolate transfer
    sheet (optional)

6. Take out of the oven and gently press out circles using 6cm cooking rings while the biscuit is still hot and malleable. Cool on a wire rack.

7. Increase the oven temperature to 190°C/170°C/gas 5. Take the Swiss roll tin out of the freezer and check that the pink stripes are frozen. Now, working quickly, spread out the remaining yellow sponge batter evenly over the tin and bake for 8 minutes. While the sponge is cooking, cut a piece of baking parchment big enough to turn the sponge out on. Lay it on a cooling rack and sprinkle with a little caster sugar to stop the sponge from sticking to it when turned out.

8. Take the sponge out of the oven and use a small knife to release it from the edges of the baking parchment. Turn it out on to your sugar-coated paper and peel off the now-exposed baking parchment from the base of the tin. Leave to cool completely.

9. Make the rhubarb filling by chopping the rhubarb and heating in a saucepan with the butter, sugar and cornflour. Stir occasionally to stop the mixture from sticking to the pan. Cook for about 10 minutes until the rhubarb has broken down and the mixture has become sticky. Scrape into a small bowl and put in the fridge to cool.

10. Lay the sponge on a chopping board and, with a ruler as a guide, cut off the ragged edges. Cut out 6 strips of patterned sponge, each 17 x 3cm. Put the cooking rings on a baking tray and lay the cooled biscuit bases in them, then curl up the sponge strips (striped side out) and fit them inside the rings, gently pressing them down.

11. Turn the custard into crème pâtissière by whisking the double cream in a bowl until soft peaks form, then folding it into the now-cooled custard 1 tbsp at a time. Load it into a piping bag fitted with a long-nosed nozzle and gently pipe a thin layer into each entremet case on top of the biscuit and around the inside of the sponge layer, but leave a small area for the rhubarb filling in the centre (see opposite). Do not pipe above the sponge layer.

12. Spoon some of the cooled rhubarb into the small indent in the custard (this should be about 1½ tsp for each cake). Put the entremets in the fridge (still on their baking tray) to firm up for 30 minutes.

13. To make the ginger cream, spoon the mascarpone and double cream into a bowl and whisk together using the electric whisk until combined, but not yet thickened. Add the icing sugar and ginger and whisk until the cream thickens up.

14. Take the entremets out of the fridge and, using a small offset palette knife, fill the cases up to the top with ginger cream, making sure not to leave any hollow areas at the bottom. Use the palette knife to form as flat a surface as you can on the cream and put the entremets in the freezer for 1 hour.

Continued...

15. Make the jelly by chopping the rhubarb into 1cm lengths and cooking over a low heat with the sugar and 5 tbsp of water. Cook for 10–15 minutes, mashing it up with a spoon occasionally, until the rhubarb has gone soft and sloppy. Put the gelatine in a cup with some cold water to soften it up.

16. Once the rhubarb has disintegrated, strain through a sieve into a bowl. You may need a spoon to push the juice out of the rhubarb, but don't worry – it won't give you a cloudy jelly like it can with other fruit. Drain the gelatine and stir it into the rhubarb water until it dissolves. Depending on how pink your rhubarb is, you may want to add a little pink food colour.

17. Take the entremets out of the freezer and – using the flat plunger that comes with your entremet rings, or improvising with another 6cm-diameter flat-surfaced object – push the ginger cream down about 2–3mm. The biscuit base will start to push out of the bottom of the entremet ring, so be careful that it doesn't fall off. You may need to warm the outside edge of the ring with your hands to allow the cake to slide through. Pour the jelly on top of the cream layer of each entremet and chill in the fridge for at least an hour to set.

18. If you want to make the chocolate finishing touches, melt half the white chocolate in a heatproof bowl over a saucepan of water (don't let the water touch the bowl). While it is melting, finely chop the remaining 50g of white chocolate. As soon as the chocolate has melted, take off the heat and stir in half of the chopped chocolate. If this melts in fully in under 30 seconds, leave it for 5 minutes before stirring in the rest of the chocolate. Once all the chocolate is stirred in, spread it over the chocolate transfer sheet with the offset palette knife and leave to set at room temperature.

19. Take the entremets out of the fridge and release them from their rings by pushing up with your fingers on the biscuit base (once again, you may need to warm the outside of the rings with your hands to get the entremets to move).

20. Peel away the film from the chocolate transfers and stick these into the top of the jelly layer. Collapse with pride!

Extras

If, by the end of this book, you're confident enough to tackle these entremets, I reckon you might not need me to suggest what you fancy doing next! These circular, layered and encased little cakes encapsulate most of the skills you need to construct whatever bake you feel like making. The things to remember with them are precision and scale. Keep everything neat and maintain the proportions of the layers: try to keep the layers defined, then top with beautiful jellies, candied fruits or tempered chocolate. Have fun and be creative. And, thank you for buying my book!

BASICS

12

MINCEMEAT

Once you can make mincemeat, you can have an unending supply of mince pies! If you're vegetarian, replace the beef suet with vegetable suet, or if you're not into suet at all, melt 225g of unsalted butter and stir that into the mix instead (this is actually quite delicious).

MAKES ABOUT 1.6KG /
4 JARS

Ingredients

225g cooking apples

225g currants

225g raisins

225g sultanas

100g candied mixed peel

finely grated zest of 2 oranges
    and 2 unwaxed lemons

100ml brandy

100ml almond liqueur, such
    as amaretto

225g shredded beef suet

2 tsp mixed spice

1 tsp freshly grated nutmeg

200g dark brown
    muscovado sugar

Tool Kit

4 empty jam jars with lids

4 waxed paper discs
    (available online)

1. Chop the apples into tiny cubes (less than 1cm) and put in a large bowl with the currants, raisins, sultanas, mixed peel and zests. Pour the brandy and liqueur over the fruit and mix with a wooden spoon until all the fruit is coated in booze. Cover with cling film and leave for at least 6 hours for the fruit to plump up.

2. Tip in the suet, spices and sugar and mix well with a wooden spoon. Leave to stand overnight, stirring occasionally every now and then (don't stay up half the night; before bed and in the morning will do).

3. Sterilise 4 empty jam jars with lids – a hot wash in the dishwasher will be fine for this – and spoon the mincemeat into them. Lay a waxed paper disc in each jar and seal it. This lasts for ages... my jars go on at least until next year and the year after that.

Extras

Swap out the liqueur content, if you like, with whatever feels Christmassy to you. I'm always a sucker for sticking Grand Marnier in mine, but try not to lose the brandy as, for some reason, it just tastes wrong without it. Muck about with the fruit here, too. Swap in dried cranberries, sour cherries or chopped apricots if you want a nice sharp note; just maintain the same total weight of fruit and you'll be fine. Happy Christmas!

HONEYCOMB

A bag of honeycomb takes me right back to trips to the fair as a kid. These days I make it on a strictly rationed basis, just because if I've got it in the house it's going to get eaten pretty quickly! Honeycomb is very easy to make, so I definitely recommend it if you're bored of a Saturday afternoon, or to make to nibble on if you're having a party. (*Pictured on pages 214–215.*)

MAKES A SMALL ROASTING TINFUL

Ingredients
75ml golden syrup
250g caster sugar
1 tbsp bicarbonate of soda

Tool Kit
small roasting tin (mine is
    26 x 23cm)

1. Line a small roasting tin (mine is 26 x 23cm) with baking parchment. The paper needs to come up to the top of the tin at least.

2. Put a saucepan on your kitchen scales, set them to zero, and pour in the golden syrup (this is my favourite method of weighing out sticky ingredients). Add the sugar to the saucepan and set it over a medium heat.

3. Once melted together, continue to heat until the mixture starts to turn light brown. As soon as the colour changes, spoon in the bicarbonate of soda and mix it in. The mixture will foam up at this point and turn yellow.

4. Carefully pour into the roasting tin (*it will be very hot!*) and leave to cool for 1 hour or until it has set.

5. Turn out of the tin and crack up into bite-sized chunks for serving, keeping the crumbs for yourself; you did make it, after all!

Extras
Because honeycomb is heated up so much, adding flavour can be fairly tricky, so I like to coat mine after they cool instead. Melt about 100g dark chocolate (70 per cent cocoa solids) and either pour on top of your uncracked (cooled) honeycomb, then break up once it is set, or roll cracked shards of honeycomb into the melted chocolate. This will taste lovely, and stop the honeycomb going sticky in the open air. You can also colour the honeycomb, by adding gel food colour to the cold mix and cooking as above. Red colours work well with the honeycomb's golden base colour. Use lots of colour for vivid-toned shards; it looks brilliant!

COCONUT MARSHMALLOWS

When I found out how to make marshmallows in my own kitchen, a childish delight must have descended on me for about two or three weeks! The amazing wobble you get from home-made marshmallows is a sight to behold, while the flavours you can put into them take them well beyond the offerings you can pick up in a plastic bag in the supermarket. Please have a go at making these; they are a pure joy! *(Pictured overleaf.)*

MAKES A SMALL ROASTING TINFUL

Ingredients
12 leaves of gelatine
500g caster sugar
1 tsp vanilla bean paste
400g desiccated coconut
pink gel food colour

Tool Kit
small roasting tin (mine is
    26 x 23cm)
stand mixer fitted with
    whisk (optional)
electric whisk (optional)
small sandwich bags
    (optional)

1. Start by lining a small roasting tin (mine is 26 x 23cm) with baking parchment, to at least the top edge of the tin. Cut up the gelatine leaves with scissors and soak in a small bowl with 120ml of water.

2. Pour the sugar and 120ml more water into a saucepan and set over a medium heat until the sugar dissolves. Add the softened gelatine (and the soaking water) and bring to the boil, stirring until all the gelatine dissolves. Pour the hot liquid into the bowl of a stand mixer fitted with a whisk attachment (or a large bowl if you are using an electric whisk). Leave to cool for at least 45 minutes.

3. Whisk on high for 10 minutes until a thick foam has formed. (If you are using an electric whisk, this will take about 15 minutes, but persevere – it will thicken up!) Pour into the prepared tin and leave to set. This will take ages, probably overnight, but at least 6 hours.

4. Once the marshmallow has set (the top surface will still stick to your hands), gently lift it out of the tin, still in the baking parchment. Lay it on a work surface and carefully cut the marshmallow away from the parchment using a sharp knife dipped in water. (A wet knife is essential here, to stop the marshmallow ripping when you cut it.)

5. For the pink coconut, put half the desiccated coconut into a sandwich bag and add a small amount of gel colour. Tease the colour through the coconut by rubbing the bag between your fingers. Or try mixing in the colour by hand in a bowl. For the white coconut, just add the remaining coconut to another bag, or put in a bowl.

6. Using the wet knife again, cut the marshmallow block into pieces about 4 x 3cm. Pick them up (without touching the top surface) and roll them in the coconut (either in the sandwich bag or in a bowl). It will stick to the outside of the marshmallows. *Try to share them.*

Extras
Marshmallows can really take flavour. Have fun with them by adding extracts to the syrup: 1 tsp of rose or peppermint can taste brilliant! Add pulped fruit for fruity marshmallows: blackcurrant and raspberry work well as the sharpness of the fruit can cut through the massive amount of sugar, and the colours come through, too. Just remember to replace the water with fruit pulp, rather than adding any more liquid, or your marshmallows will never set!

Roll them in hundreds and thousands, blitzed pralines, popping candy, or 75g of icing sugar mixed with 75g of cornflour for a more traditional marshmallow.

PEPPERMINT TURKISH DELIGHT

LEVEL 2

For the last 80 years, all the builders in my family have had lunch on a Friday afternoon in the same café. The café has been through at least four owners during my tenure alone, leaving us and our fellow builders as pretty much the only constant fixture. Next to this café is a Turkish supermarket, where my dad and I buy all our treats for the weekend: usually exotic fruit, baklava and loads of flavours of Turkish delight. This recipe only scrapes the surface of a sweet on which you could write a whole book! *(Pictured on prevous page.)*

MAKES A SMALL ROASTING TINFUL
Ingredients
a few drops of vegetable oil
600g caster sugar
1 tbsp lemon juice
145g cornflour
2 tsp peppermint extract
blue liquid food colour (not
    gel food colour)
green liquid food colour
    (not gel food colour)
25g icing sugar

Tool Kit
small baking tin or dish
    (mine is 23 x 15cm)
pastry brush
confectionery thermometer
electric whisk (optional)
offset palette knife

1. Line a small, baking tin or dish (mine is 23 x 15cm) with baking parchment, then brush the paper with a little oil.

2. Mix the caster sugar, lemon juice and 220ml water in a saucepan over a medium heat. Add a confectionery thermometer and bring the temperature to 118°C ('soft ball' stage on some thermometers).

3. Meanwhile, mix 120g of the cornflour in a large saucepan with 380ml of water. When the syrup reaches the soft ball stage, take it off the heat, then place the cornflour mixture over a medium heat (the syrup needs a few minutes to cool down or it turns the mix lumpy).

4. As the cornflour mixture begins to warm up, mix with a whisk – this is easier with an electric whisk but perfectly possible with a manual version; it will thicken up as it heats.

5. Once the cornflour has formed a thick paste, pour in one-quarter of the syrup and beat until smooth. Continue to beat in the remaining syrup, one-quarter at a time, until it is all incorporated. Do not mix in all the syrup at once, or the mixture will turn lumpy.

6. Reduce the heat to as low as it will go and heat for 45 minutes, stirring every 2–3 minutes to stop it burning. The mixture should get thicker and turn slightly yellow.

7. Stir in the peppermint extract thoroughly. Add food colour; I use about 20 drops of blue and 5 drops of green, but add it in increments and use your judgement to get the colour you want.

8. Pour the mixture into the prepared tin or dish and smooth out with a palette knife. Leave to cool and set overnight, or for at least 6 hours.

9. Once set, mix the remaining cornflour and the icing sugar and use 1 tbsp of it to dust the top of the Turkish delight. Turn the slab out on a clean work surface and spoon more cornflour mixture over.

10. Cut into 2–3cm squares and dust with the cornflour mixture. Eat!

Extras
Make traditional Turkish delight using 1 tsp of rose water and a few drops of red food colour. Or add 100g of chopped pistachios (after 45 minutes of mixing) and flavour with rose water or 2 tbsp of lemon juice. Or pour in 3 tbsp of runny honey and add pistachios or toasted almonds. Experiment with orange blossom water, finely grated citrus zests and preserved ginger.

FRANGIPANE

If I could get away with it, I would shoehorn frangipane into just about everything I eat. The flavour of caramelised, sugary almond – whether it's in Bakewell tarts or croissants – can be just magical. Have a go at this recipe, get the hang of it, and then become as addicted to it as I am. It's wonderful spread on a puff pastry tart, with fruit baked into the top.

MAKES ENOUGH FOR A 23CM TART

Ingredients

200g unsalted butter, at room temperature
200g caster sugar
½ tsp almond extract
4 large eggs
2 tbsp plain flour
200g ground almonds

Tool Kit

electric whisk
piping bag (optional)

1. Beat the butter and sugar together with an electric whisk until light-coloured and fluffy; this should take a few minutes.

2. Add the almond extract and beat the eggs in thoroughly, one at a time, adding some of the flour if it starts to split.

3. Fold in the remaining flour and the ground almonds until a smooth, even paste forms.

4. Load into a piping bag, or transfer to a bowl and cover with cling film, until ready to use.

Extras

There – couldn't be easier really. One of my favourite things to make with this is a plum Bakewell tart. Simply use a sweet pastry base (see page 128) in a 23cm tart tin. Spread plum jam in the base of the tart case, pipe on the frangipane and poke in sliced greengages. Bake at 190°C/fan 170°C/gas 5 for 50-60 minutes, or until the top becomes nicely browned. Delicious!

ACKNOWLEDGEMENTS

Writing books is hard! When I first embarked on this, I thought it would just be a few weeks of mucking around in the kitchen, followed by another few weeks of tapping away at a keyboard. Boy, was I wrong. It took over my life! I have loved every minute of it, even though I did become a hermit for several months.

First and foremost I would like to thank my wife Sarah, for giving me the nudge to go on the *Bake-Off* in the first place, for helping me organise everything, and for never giving up helping me with recipes even at 2 a.m. on a school night! I love you, sweetheart.

Thanks to my lovely daughters, Elizabeth and Genevieve. I hope this has left some fond memories for the pair of you. I love you both so much, and I promise we'll make cookies whenever you want.

I'd like to thank my dad and business partner, Peter. Thanks, Dad, for keeping things going while I've been pretty unreliable. I'll be back soon.

My mum, Adrienne, for showing me how to cook in the first place, for looking after the kids and for secretly nipping into my kitchen and clearing up while I napped.

Thank you to my two sisters, Joanne and Katherine, for moral support, rearranging my larder and dedicated testing of hundreds of bakes.

To all the rest of the family: Trent, James, Jamie, Vicky, Kate, Karsten, Fran and Joe. Thanks for the recipe ideas and endless enthusiasm for the book.

Thanks to Ed, Dawn, Helena, Glyn and Helen, Damon and Therese, Hayley and Jon, Louise and Max, Priya and Alex, Sarah's team at work, everyone at my daughter's nursery, the staff at my sister's work and our babysitter Charlotte. Your tasting, feedback and advice have been invaluable.

Thank you to Rosemary and Aoife at United Agents: your astute support and friendship have been an exciting surprise to a tradesman lost among the media.

Thanks to the *Bake-Off* Class of 2014: Claire, Enwezor, Jordan, Iain, Diana, Norman, Kate, Martha, Chetna, Luis, Nancy and all the team at Love Productions for your friendship over the past crazy year.

Thanks to Helen Lewis, Sarah Lavelle and all at Quadrille. The support and creativity you have shown have been a massive revelation to me. I honestly had no idea there was so much craft and hard work involved in a book. Thanks also to Lucy Bannell for being such a patient editor.

Thanks to Chris Terry and Danny for making my food look better on screen than it did 3 feet away in real life.

Thanks to Emily Jonzen. By far the best chef/stylist/posh girl in the room.

Thanks to Polly Webb-Wilson for creativity, ideas, props, and giant boxes of stuff in the study.

Thanks to Rukmini Iyer for the skills and the reality experience.

And finally, thanks to Leia, my daft dog. How you have not contracted dog diabetes from hoovering up everything on the floor, I'll never know. Let's go down to the woods for a walk...

INDEX

A

almond
  almond crust 151–3
  almond pastry 144
  cherry and almond
    Swiss roll 55–7
  frangipane 217
  'free from' orange and
    almond cake 77
  marzipan 61–3
anise and fig millefeuille
  189–91
apple
  apple and cinnamon
    Chelsea buns 38–40
  apple strudel 184–5
asparagus and bacon tart
  146–7

B

bacon
  asparagus and bacon tart
    146–7
  expedition pie 121–3
  individual pork pies 118–20
  leftover chicken pie 110–11
baklava, rose and pistachio
  174–5
banoffee tartlets 148–50
beef
  beef Wellington 168–71
  chilli con carne pasties
    164–7
  steak and ale pie 112–14
biscuit bases
  key lime pie 132–3
  pink grapefruit cheesecake
    140–1

rhubarb and custard
  entremets 205–9
biscuits
  blackcurrant macarons
    100–1
  building a cabin in the
    woods 102–7
  chocolate orange biscotti
    dunkers 98–9
  coconut macaroons 90–1
  fennel seeded thins 95
  lavender shortbread 92–3
  lemon curd sandwich
    biscuits 96–7
  peanut butter building site
    cookies 94
black forest gateau 85–7
blackberry, elderflower and
  mint pavlovas 200–1
blackcurrant macarons 100–1
bloomer, simple white 14–16
blueberry, patisserie fruit
  tart 151–3
brandy buttercream 58–9
bread
  big soft pretzels 22–3
  challah rolls 24–5
  cheeky monkey bread 42–3
  goat's cheese, walnut and
    pear pinwheel 26–9
  green olive and rosemary
    focaccia 20–1
  pizza 12–13
  seeded wholemeal rolls
    16, 18
  simple white bloomer 14–16
bread and butter pud, posh
  204
breadsticks, black olive and
  rosemary 17, 19
brioche

brioche burger buns 32–3
  posh bread and butter
    pud 204
builder's quiche 145
building a cabin in the
  woods 102–7
buns
  apple and cinnamon
    Chelsea 38–40
  brioche burger 32–3
buttercream 73–4
  brandy 58–9
  Italian meringue 64–7
butternut squash, expedition
  pie 121–3
butterscotch sauce 198–9

C

cakes
  cherry and almond Swiss
    roll 55–7
  chocolate cake 52–3
  frasier cake 61–3
  hazelnut chocolate opera
    cake 64–7
  Jamaican ginger cake 54
  mincemeat cupcakes 58–9
  pineapple upside-down
    cake 60
  Victoria sponge 50–1
  see also celebration cakes
caramel
  caramel filling 148–50
  caramel sauce 42–3
  caramel topping 38–40
cardamom and white
  chocolate éclairs 178–9
celebration cakes
  black forest gateau 85–7
  Christmas cake 78–81
  'free from' orange and

almond cake 77
lemon and poppy seed
 birthday cake 70–2
Madeira cake with fondant
 decorating techniques
 73–5
peach and white chocolate
 ombré cake 82–4
Simnel cake 76
challah rolls 24–5
cheeky monkey bread 42–3
cheese straws 157
cheesecake, pink grapefruit
 140–1
Chelsea buns, apple and
 cinnamon 38–40
cherry
 black forest gateau 85–7
 cherry and almond Swiss
  roll 55–7
 cherry and peach pie 134–5
chicken
 expedition pie 121–3
 leftover chicken pie 110–11
chilli con carne pasties 164–7
chipolatas, mushroom and
 tomato tea-break Danish
 161–3
chocolate
 black forest gateau 85–7
 chocolate cake 52–3
 chocolate ganache 52–3, 64–7
 chocolate oozing puddings
  202–3
 chocolate orange biscotti
  dunkers 98–9
 chocolate passion fruit
  ganache 186–8
 coconut macaroons 90–1
 decorating with chocolate
  85–7

hazelnut chocolate opera
 cake 64–7
Irish cream profiteroles 177
pains au chocolat 186–8
sweet chocolate pastry
 148–50
choux pastry
 basic 176
 Irish cream profiteroles 177
 white chocolate and
  cardamom éclairs 178–9
Christmas cake 78–81
cinnamon and apple Chelsea
 buns 38–40
coconut
 coconut macaroons 90–1
 coconut marshmallows
  213–15
coffee syrup 64–7
cookies, peanut butter
 building site 94
coulis, raspberry 202–3
cream cheese frosting 70–2
 white chocolate 82–4
crème brûlée, orange
 blossom 196–7
crème pâtissière 61–3, 151–3
 orange 178–9
croissants 180–1
cupcakes, mincemeat 58–9
curd
 lemon 142–3
 lime 142–3
 orange 77
custard 189–91
 custard tart 144
 pouring custard 136–7
 rhubarb and custard
  entremets 205–9

D

Danish pastry dough
 croissants 180–1
 pains au chocolat 186–8
 plum Danish 182–3
 sausage, mushroom and
  tomato tea-break Danish
  161–3
date(s), sticky toffee pudding
 198–9
doughnuts
 double-glazed ring
  doughnuts 34–5
 jam doughnuts 36–7
dried fruit
 apple strudel 184–5
 Christmas cake 78–81
 posh bread and butter
  pud 204
 mincemeat 211
 panettone 41
 Simnel cake 76
 Swedish wreath 44–7

E

éclairs, white chocolate and
 cardamom 178–9
egg 9
elderflower, blackberry and
 mint pavlovas 200–1
entremets, rhubarb and
 custard 205–9
equipment 8–9
expedition pie 121–3

F

fennel
 fennel seeded thins 95
 pork, fennel and chilli
  sausage rolls 158–60
feta, expedition pie 121–3

fig and anise millefeuille 189–91
filo pastry
   lamb samosas 156
   rose and pistachio baklava
     174–5
fish dishes, sea-fisherman's
   pie 115–17
flour 9
focaccia, green olive and
   rosemary 20–1
fondant decorating
   techniques 73–5
food colourings 9
frangipane 217
frasier cake 61–3
'free from' orange and
   almond cake 77
French meringue 194
fresh cream
   banoffee tartlets 148–50
   black forest gateau 85–7
   cherry and almond Swiss
     roll 55–7
   Irish cream profiteroles 177
   Victoria sponge 50–1
frosting see cream cheese
   frosting

G

ganache
   chocolate passion fruit
186–8
   dark chocolate 52–3, 64–7
   white chocolate 178–9
ginger
   ginger mascarpone 206–9
   gingerbread (building a
     cabin in the woods) 102–7
   Jamaican ginger cake 54
glazes, for doughnuts 34–5
goat's cheese, walnut and

pear pinwheel 26–9
grapefruit see pink
   grapefruit cheesecake

H

hazelnut chocolate opera
   cake 64–7
honeycomb 212, 214–15
hot water crust 112–14, 118–23

I

icing
   fondant decorating
     techniques 73–5
   royal 78–81, 102–7
   see also cream cheese
     frosting
ingredients 9
Irish cream profiteroles 177
Italian meringue 195
Italian meringue
   buttercream 64–7

J

jam
   jam doughnuts 36–7
   plum Danish 182–3
   strawberry jam 50–1, 142–3
   traffic light jam tarts 142–3
   Victoria sponge 50–1
Jamaican ginger cake 54
jelly
   for expedition pie 121–3
   for pork pies 118–20
   rhubarb jelly 206–9
   strawberry jelly 62–3

K

key lime pie 132–3
kiwi, patisserie fruit tart
   151–3

L

lamb samosas 156
lavender shortbread 92–3
lemon
   lemon curd 142–3
   lemon curd sandwich
     biscuits 96–7
   lemon and poppy seed
birthday cake 70–2
lime
   key lime pie 132–3
   lime curd 142–3

M

macarons, blackcurrant
   100–1
macaroons, coconut 90–1
Madeira cake with fondant
   decorating techniques 73–5
marshmallows, coconut
   213–15
marzipan
   Christmas cake 78–81
   plum Danish 182–3
   recipe 61–3
mascarpone, ginger 206–9
meringue
   blackberry, elderflower and
     mint pavlovas 200–1
   blackcurrant macarons
     100–1
   French meringue 194
   Italian meringue 195
   Italian meringue
     buttercream 64–7
   key lime pie 132–3
millefeuille, fig and anise
   189–91
mince pies 128–9
mincemeat 211
   mincemeat cupcakes 58–9

mint, blackberry and elderflower pavlovas 200–1
mushroom
    beef Wellington 168–71
    sausage, mushroom and tomato tea-break Danish 161–3
    steak and ale pie 112–14

O

olive
    black olive and rosemary breadsticks 17, 19
    green olive and rosemary focaccia 20–1
opera cake, hazelnut chocolate 64–7
orange
    chocolate orange biscotti dunkers 98–9
    posh bread and butter pud 204
    'free from' orange and almond cake 77
    orange crème pâtissière 178–9
    orange curd 77
    white chocolate and cardamom éclairs 178–9
orange blossom crème brûlée 196–7

P

pains au chocolat 186–8
panettone 41
    posh bread and butter pud 204
passion fruit chocolate ganache 186–8
pasties, chilli con carne 164–7

pastry 126–7, 134–5, 142–3
    almond crust 151–3
    almond pastry 144
    cheese straws 157
    choux pastry 176–9
    Danish pastry dough 161–3, 180–3, 186–8
    filo pastry 156, 174–5
    hot water crust 112–14, 118–23
    puff pastry 115–17, 146–7, 168–71, 184–5, 189–91
    rich rough puff pastry 158–60
    rough puff pastry 164–7
    shortcrust pastry 110–11, 145
    sweet chocolate pastry 148–50
    sweet shortcrust pastry 128–31
patisserie fruit tart 151–3
pavlovas, blackberry, elderflower and mint 200–1
peach
    cherry and peach pie 134–5
    peach purée 82–4
    peach and white chocolate ombré cake 82–4
peanut butter building site cookies 94
pear, goat's cheese and walnut pinwheel 26–9
pecan pie with spiced rum 130–1
peppermint Turkish delight 214–16
pesto, expedition pie 121–3
pies
    cherry and peach pie 134–5
    expedition pie 121–3

individual pork pies 118–20
key lime pie 132–3
leftover chicken pie 110–11
mince pies 128–9
pecan pie with spiced rum 130–1
plum pie 126–7
sea-fisherman's pie 115–17
steak and ale pie 112–14
pineapple upside-down cake 60
pink grapefruit cheesecake 140–1
pinwheel, goat's cheese, walnut and pear 26–9
pistachio
    pistachio sponge 61–3
    pistachio syrup 61–3
    rose and pistachio baklava 174–5
pizza 12–13
plum
    plum Danish 182–3
    plum pie 126–7
pomegranate seeds, pink grapefruit cheesecake 140–1
poppy seed and lemon birthday cake 70–2
pork
    fennel and chilli sausage rolls 158–60
    individual pork pies 118–20
praline 64–7
prawn, sea-fisherman's pie 115–17
pretzels, big soft 22–3
profiteroles, Irish cream 177
puff pastry
    apple strudel 184–5
    asparagus and bacon tart 146–7

beef Wellington 168–71
fig and anise millefeuille
189–91
sea-fisherman's pie 115–17
see also rich rough puff
pastry; rough puff pastry

Q

quiche, builder's 145

R

raspberry
jam doughnuts 36–7
patisserie fruit tart 151–3
raspberry coulis 202–3
red kidney bean(s), chilli con
carne pasties 164–7
rhubarb
rhubarb and custard
entremets 205–9
rhubarb jelly 206–9
rich rough puff pastry 158–60
rose and pistachio baklava
174–5
rough puff pastry 164–7
see also rich rough puff
pastry
royal icing
building a cabin in the
woods 102–7
Christmas cake 78–81
rum (spiced), pecan pie with
130–1

S

salt 9
samosas, lamb 156
sausage, mushroom and
tomato tea-break Danish
161–3
sausagemeat

individual pork pies 118–20
pork, fennel and chilli
sausage rolls 158–60
sea-fisherman's pie 115–17
seeded wholemeal rolls 16, 18
shortbread, lavender 92–3
shortcrust pastry
builder's quiche 145
leftover chicken pie 110–11
sweet shortcrust pastry
128–31
steak and ale pie 112–14
sticky toffee pudding 198–9
Stilton cheese, builder's
quiche 145
strawberry
frasier cake 61–3
patisserie fruit tart 151–3
strawberry jam 50–1, 142–3
strawberry jelly 62–3
strudel, apple 184–5
Swedish wreath 44–7
sweet shortcrust pastry
128–31
Swiss roll, cherry and
almond 55–7

T

tarts
asparagus and bacon tart
146–7
banoffee tartlets 148–50
custard tart 144
patisserie fruit tart 151–3
traffic light jam tarts 142–3
tear-and-share cheeky
monkey bread 42–3
thins, fennel seeded 95
toffee, sticky toffee pudding
198–9
tomato

chilli con carne pasties
164–7
pizza sauce 12–13
sausage, mushroom and
tomato tea-break Danish
161–3
tool kit 8–9
traffic light jam tarts 142–3
Turkish delight, peppermint
214–16

V

Victoria sponge 50–1

W

walnut
expedition pie 121–3
goat's cheese, walnut and
pear pinwheel 26–9
water 9
Wellington, beef 168–71
white chocolate
peach and white chocolate
ombré cake 82–4
rhubarb and custard
entremets 206–9
white chocolate and
cardamom éclairs 178–9
white chocolate frosting
82–4
white chocolate ganache
178–9
wreath, Swedish 44–7

Y

yeast 9